INSTITUTE OF LEADERSHIP & MANAGEMENT ilm

SUPERSERIES

Understanding Finance

FOURTH EDITION

GW00496876

Published for the
Institute of Leadership & Management by **Pergamon** *Flexible* **Learning**

OXFORD   AMSTERDAM   BOSTON   LONDON   NEW YORK   PARIS
SAN DIEGO   SAN FRANCISCO   SINGAPORE   SYDNEY   TOKYO

Pergamon Flexible Learning
An imprint of Elsevier Science
Linacre House, Jordan Hill, Oxford OX2 8DP
200 Wheeler Road, Burlington, MA 01803

First published 1986
Second edition 1991
Third edition 1997
Fourth edition 2003

Copyright © 1986, 1991, 1997, 2003, ILM
All rights reserved.

No part of this publication may be reproduced in any material form (including
photocopying or storing in any medium by electronic means and whether
or not transiently or incidentally to some other use of this publication) without
the written permission of the copyright holder except in accordance with the
provisions of the Copyright, Designs and Patents Act 1988 or under the terms
of a licence issued by the Copyright Licensing Agency Ltd, 90 Tottenham Court Road, London,
England W1T 4LP. Applications for the copyright holder's written
permission to reproduce any part of this publication should be addressed
to the publisher

British Library Cataloguing in Publication Data
A catalogue record for this book is available from the British Library

ISBN 0 7506 5815 0

For information on Pergamon Flexible Learning
visit our website at www.bh.com/pergamonfl

Institute of Leadership & Management
registered office
1 Giltspur Street
London
EC1A 9DD
Telephone 020 7294 3053
www.i-l-m.com
ILM is a subsidiary of the City & Guilds Group

The views expressed in this work are those of the authors and do
not necessarily reflect those of the Institute of Leadership &
Management or of the publisher

Authors: Raymond Taylor and Clare Donnelly
Editor: Clare Donnelly
Editorial management: Genesys, www.genesys-consultants.com
Based on previous material by: Peter Elliot
Composition by Genesis Typesetting, Rochester, Kent
Printed and bound in Great Britain by MPG Books, Bodmin

Contents

Contents

Workbook introduction

1 ILM Super Series study links

This workbook addresses the issues of *Understanding Finance*. Should you wish to extend your study to other Super Series workbooks covering related or different subject areas, you will find a comprehensive list at the back of this book.

2 Links to ILM Qualifications

This workbook relates to the following learning outcomes in segments from the ILM Level 3 Introductory Certificate in First Line Management and the Level 3 Certificate in First Line Management.

C3.2 Financial Environment
1 Recognize the importance of financial information for management.
2 Identify the main financial documents needed by the organization, and the information contained in them.
3 Recognize the most significant financial indicators of business performance and their relevance.
4 List the main sources of long, medium and short-term funds for business.

3 Links to S/NVQs in Management

This workbook relates to the following elements of the Management Standards which are used in S/NVQs in Management, as well as a range of other S/NVQs.

B1.1 Make recommendations for the use of resources
B1.2 Contribute to the control of resources
D1.1 Gather required information
D1.2 Inform and advise others.

It will also help you to develop the following Personal Competences:

■ focusing on results;
■ searching for information;
■ thinking and taking decisions.

4 Workbook objectives

As a first line manager, you may be involved in the production or sale of goods, or delivery of services.

Your performance at work, along with that of your work team, determines how well your organization does financially and how successful it is. Whether you work in a business that sets out to make a profit, or in the voluntary sector, your organization is interested in making the best use of the funds it has available. And those who supply the funds, whether they are shareholders, partners or individuals making donations, are keen to see that their money is well used. They obtain that information from year-end financial statements such as a company's annual published report and accounts. Management also needs financial information to help it run the organization day to day, and specific accounts are prepared for its use too.

In this workbook, we will look at what is included in these accounts, what they tell us and how they are used. We'll explore the way money is used in a business, and look at how performance can be measured in financial terms. Financial constraints are often very important to organizations; developing your understanding of finances will help you improve your effectiveness in the workplace. You will spot ways in which money can be better used.

Accountancy, like all specialist subjects, has its own language. Just as a car mechanic will talk of 'torque' and 'gaskets', and a computer expert will discuss 'bytes' and 'disk access time', an accountant uses expressions such as 'current liabilities' and 'retained profit'. By the end of this workbook, you will have a better appreciation of accounting vocabulary and this, in itself, will clarify what is meant by aspects of accounts that you may have found confusing and mysterious in the past.

4.1 Objectives

When you have completed this workbook you will be better able to:

- understand how important it is for any organization to have sufficient cash;
- appreciate why it is vital for an organization to control its finances by forecasting and monitoring cash flow;
- identify appropriate providers of finance in given situations;
- make sense of key financial information in profit and loss accounts and balance sheets;
- measure how well an organization is performing financially;

5 Activity planner

If you are compiling a S/NVQ portfolio, you might like to develop some of the Activities in this workbook as evidence of your competence. You may want to look at the following Activities now so that you can make prior arrangements:

Activity 21   Obtain a cash flow forecast for your organization or, if that is not possible, draw one up for a club or society in which you are involved, for yourself and your family.

Activities 31 and 37   Obtain copies of the year-end financial statements of your own organization and two or three others, say, a bank or building society, a club or charity.

Activities that may provide the basis of evidence for your S/NVQ portfolio are signposted with this icon.

The Work-based assignment (on pages 84–6) suggests that you speak to your manager, finance director or to your colleagues in the accounts office about the accounts of your organization.

You might like to start thinking now about who to approach and arrange to speak with them.

Session A
The need for accounts

1 Introduction

Money (or cash, or finance, or funds) is very important to all of us, both as private individuals and as members of organizations. It isn't that it is valuable in itself; its importance is in what it can buy and what it can do for us.

As individuals, once we've paid our tax and national insurance, how we account for our money is up to us. We may keep careful records, or we may decide to spend it while we've got it and, when it's gone, manage without.

Trading organizations, however, must keep detailed and accurate accounts if they are to stay in business at all, and if they hope to plan for the future in any meaningful way. For example, if manufacturers were approached to make a new product but did not have the right equipment to put the product together, they would have to buy new plant and machinery. If they did not know how much cash they had available, what was owing to them and how much they had to pay out in the next few weeks, how could they possibly agree to take on the contract?

There may be other reasons for turning down products than simply shortage of cash. The product might seem to have a limited market, or it might conflict with competing products already being made for other customers. Never-theless, cash is very often a critical issue.

Let's begin by looking at what money does for us.

2 How money is used

We are so familiar with money that it is easy to take it for granted and not analyse the ways in which we use it. But if you think about it, you will see the following issues.

- **Money acts as a medium of exchange.** Money enables people who make goods to obtain food, clothing and other wares. They sell their goods for money and then use the money to buy the things they need. Money enables them to exchange one thing for another.
- **Money acts as a store of wealth.** Money enables people to save or store money for 'rainy days', holidays, retirement and so on. Money is used to invest for the future.
- **Money acts as a means of deferred payment.** Money allows people to borrow and repay fixed amounts over a certain period. In other words, it allows them to buy something now, and put off or defer paying for it. They buy, say, a television now and pay for it over one or two years.
- **Money acts as a measure of values.** Money allows people to compare totally different things, such as a kilogram of apples and a pair of shoes. It is possible to do this by deciding what each is worth in money terms.

This last use of money, that enables one to apply a common measure of value to widely differing objects, is particularly useful. It means that the things you use at your workplace can be given a value in money terms, or 'costed'.

Many of the activities at your workplace can be costed, including:

- the results of your workteam's efforts;
- the use of machinery and equipment;
- the use of the buildings where you work;
- the use of the materials you work with.

Thus the cost of producing something, or providing a service, can be worked out, by using money as a measure of values. Typically if your work team paints a room, the costs of materials and labour will be added together, an element of profit will be added on and the owner of the room will be charged a price for the job.

Of course, there is a limit to translating everything into its value in money. What is a smile or a friendly word worth, for example?

Try the following questions, before you move on.

Activity 1

10 mins

You have seen that money is used in at least four ways:

a as a medium of **exchange**;
b as a **store** of wealth;
c as a means of **deferred** payment;
d as a **measure** of values.

Decide how each of the following people are using money, by circling the appropriate letter (a), (b), (c) or (d), in each situation described below. Briefly describe the reasons for your selection.

1 John has a car and a house. He decides that together they are worth £175,000. Is he thinking of money in terms of (a), (b), (c) or (d) above?

Briefly explain the reasons for your selection.

_____

_____

2 Jack has won £2,000 on the lottery, and decides to put the money into a building society until he needs it. Is he thinking of money in terms of (a), (b), (c) or (d) above?

Briefly explain the reasons for your selection.

_____

_____

3 Janet borrows £1,000 from her father to buy a car. She agrees to pay the money back at £100 a month over 10 months. Is she thinking of money in terms of (a), (b), (c) or (d) above?

Briefly explain the reasons for your selection.

_____

_____

4 Diana sells her house for £150,000 and buys a smaller house for £130,000 and a car for £20,000. Is she thinking of money in terms of (a), (b), (c) or (d) above?

Briefly explain the reasons for your selection.

_____

_____

Each situation leans towards one choice, although you may have come up with a logical reason for another choice. See how far you agree with my suggestions:

1 A car and a house are so different from each other that John can only group them together if he gives them a money value. So in this case he is using money as (d) a **measure** of values. If John's car was vintage or veteran he might combine the car and house as (b) a **store** of wealth.

   You can see that the categories are not always clear cut. Different interpretations are possible.

2 Jack is saving money to use it later, so in this case he is using money as (b) a **store** of wealth. He is also using it as an investment for the future.

3 Janet's borrowing enables her to have the car now and pay for it over a period, so she is using money as a means of (c) **deferred** payment. She will also be exchanging the cash for the car.

4 Finally, Diana is able to exchange one item, her house, for a car and a smaller house. In this case she is using money as (a) a medium of **exchange**.

   Whatever the way in which an organization uses money, it will need to record the transactions as proof of how it has used the money for all those interested in its operations.

3 The use of accounting records

Accounting records are kept by individuals, businesses, clubs, charities and non-profit organizations in order to monitor their financial positions. Accounting is the common language of business because it is used to describe the financial dealings of every kind of organization. Accounts are prepared from accounting records using the principles of accounting. We've just examined the way in which money serves a variety of purposes we can look at accounting records, accounting and accounts in the same way.

There are a number of reasons why businesses keep accounting records and prepare accounts. An organization must:

- know what it owes;
- know what it is owed;

■ know what it owns;
■ be able to examine its activities to ensure that it makes a profit or works within a budget;
■ be able to plan for the future.

In addition, certain organizations such as companies, charities and building societies are required by law to keep accounting records and prepare accounts. We will not look at legal requirements in this workbook.

The first three reasons for keeping accounting records are easily achieved by keeping a note of, or monitoring, transactions. The last two reasons are fulfilled by preparing accounts (or financial statements which we will look at later in this workbook).

3.1 Monitoring transactions

Activity 2 · 5 mins

Suppose you earn £300 per week and are paid at the end of the week. In reality you are owed £60 by the organization for which you work at the end of Monday, another £60 at the end of Tuesday and so on until Friday.

It's the same with the money you owe to others, such as the milkman and the newsagent. You may have milk and newspapers delivered, and pay what you owe at the end of the week, although bills aren't all as simple as this. Let's say that you owed the following amounts:

■ Monday £30;
■ Tuesday £35;
■ Wednesday £45;
■ Thursday £40;
■ Friday £10;
■ Saturday £20;
■ Sunday £10.

Draw up your weekly account in the following table; the first entry is shown as an example.

You will know when you have to pay for, say, your rent, as your landlord calls round at the same time each month and you make sure you have the cash available. Businesses do the same, and we will look at the timing of payments later.

	What you are owed	What you owe
Monday	£60	£30
Tuesday		
Wednesday		
Thursday		
Friday		
Saturday		
Sunday		
Totals		

The answer to this activity is on page 97.

Activity 3 ·

5 mins

Haugh Limited owes £3,000 to Punton plc. Haugh Limited does not have enough cash to pay this debt at the moment. However, it is owed £3,000 by people who have bought goods from it on credit.

How can the directors of Haugh Limited decide when they will be able to repay the debt to Punton plc?

_____

_____

_____

The directors of Haugh Limited would want to know when the £3,000 it is owed will be paid. Until the cash comes in from its customers, it will clearly not be available to pass it on to Punton plc. So the directors will need to know the various dates when the cash will be coming in, particularly when the full amount is to be received. The directors can then promise Punton plc that they will be paid after a particular date. Of course, Haugh Limited will then be relying on its customers paying up when they say they will.

Organizations could have a number of debts and be owed money for many sales. This makes it even more important for its accounting records to be accurate so that they can manage to pay debts on time whenever possible.

Activity 4

5 mins

Suppose Punton plc is not happy with the proposals suggested by the directors of Haugh Limited and is pressing for payment. Punton plc wants the £3,000 owed now. What can the directors of Haugh Limited do? Try to think of two things the company might do if it does not yet have the money to pay Punton plc.

_____

_____

_____

_____

There are a number of possibilities you may have suggested, including the following.

- The company could default by not paying what it owes. (Not recommended!)
- It could borrow the money – it would then still owe £3,000, but to the bank, not Punton plc.
- It could sell something it owns – it could sell £3,000 worth of goods, or sell off a piece of land or equipment, for immediate payment so that it can pay the money on to Punton plc.

This suggests that the following are closely connected in the accounting records of Haugh Limited in this case:

- how much is **owned** by the company;
- how much is **owed** by the company;
- how much is **owed** to the company.

This applies equally to all organizations. A care provider must pay employees, business rates and other expenses on time; a charity may need to finance a homeless shelter by a specific date. And you can imagine the effects of the cash not being available at the right time on the customers and clients of such organizations.

3.2 Working to a budget

Now let's look at our fourth reason why a company keeps accounting records: to be able to examine its activities to ensure that it makes a profit or works within a budget. Again we'll take an example.

Activity 5

3 mins

Suppose your take-home pay this month is £1,000 and you have to make the following payments:

- housekeeping £400;
- mortgage £300;
- insurance £100;
- car loan £250.

It's clear that you don't have enough money to meet all your monthly payments. You are going to be short by £50.

From our last activity we know you could try to borrow the £50, or you could default on one of your payments, but this would be foolish! Next month, you'd have a worse problem – you would be £50 short again and also owe £50.

Make a brief note of how you might deal with this problem.

_____

_____

_____

It seems apparent that your income must rise or your spending must be reduced. You could do this by, for example:

- selling your car – if it covers the outstanding loan;
- cancelling your insurance – or changing to cheaper cover;
- cutting down on housekeeping;
- remortgaging so as to get a better rate of interest.

In order to avoid long-term debt your income must exceed your expenditure, and the same applies to any organization. In the long term no organization can survive if the money it receives – whether this be from sales, grants or, even a donation from those who distribute the funds of the National Lottery – is less than the money it spends.

3.3 Making a profit

We can see that an organization cannot survive unless it has enough income to pay its expenses. So the fourth reason why a business must keep accounting records is to enable it to examine its day-to-day activities to ensure that it makes an excess of income over expenditure – known as a profit – or at least works within its budget.

Profit = Total income – Total expenditure

Organizations that do not make a profit will need to ensure that at the worst:

Total income = Total expenditure

This ensures survival. Often non-profit organizations will want to make a surplus, which is their equivalent of a profit. The difference is they don't usually have shareholders to pay dividends to, so the surplus is money for a 'rainy day'.

Activity 6

2 mins

Suggest a couple of additional reasons why an organization should wish to make a profit or surplus.

_____

_____

There are various possibilities you may have suggested, such as:

■ to provide money to pay out to the owners as a reward for financing a business;
■ to build up money to replace equipment and machinery as it wears out;
■ to help the organization expand.

3.4 Planning

Suppose your monthly take-home pay is £1,000 and your monthly expenses are £950. This enables you to save £50 per month. Next year, you may want to go abroad on holiday, which will cost you £850. However, in the next twelve months you can only save £600.

In the same way, an organization's plans have to be based upon realistic forecasts of the money it will have available. And you saw from the last activity how important generating profits is in helping to put plans into action.

This is the fifth reason for keeping accounting records: to make it possible to plan for the future in a practical way.

Activity 7

5 mins

Amos Phiri expects his business to generate a profit of £42,000 in the next year and there are several ways he could deal with the profit:

1   he could pay his employees a bonus of 10% of their annual wages, which will cost £36,000;

2   he could buy himself a BMW car for £38,000;

3   he could purchase new machinery for £40,000 which it is expected will generate a further £10,000 profit each year;

4   he could keep all the profit in the bank in a deposit account just in case the business is less successful in the future.

Write down one point for and one point against each of the above possible courses of action.

1   For   _____

Against   _____

2   For   _____

Against   _____

3 For _____

  Against _____

4 For _____

  Against _____

There are a number of points you may have suggested. For instance, a bonus to employees might well encourage loyalty and retain staff, and they might work harder for Amos. But they might expect to receive a bonus in future years, and even include an amount for a bonus in their annual household budget. Or, they may feel that it would be better to include the amount in wages in future. Much depends on the present relationship between Amos and his employees.

As the business belongs to Amos, he would be within his rights to take out the money and buy a BMW. Clearly this would benefit him. But this might well cause resentment among the workforce who helped to generate the profit.

In both of the first two examples, money is going out of the business for good, and if the next year is not as successful, this could mean it gets into financial difficulties without anything to 'fall back on'.

The idea of purchasing more machinery to generate additional profits is attractive for the business and, if employees see this as a signal of job security, it could be well received by them too. If the plans are successful, there will be more to share out in the future. But, it does mean deferring rewards for employees and the owner to some future time. And both Amos and his workers might like some money now.

Finally, keeping the profit in a bank deposit account would help in case of future financial difficulties. The business would be able to pay its debts even if sufficient money was not coming in day to day. But a greater profit is likely to be made if Amos uses the money in the business than would be obtained from interest paid on a deposit account.

Whenever a business makes plans, there will be disadvantages as well as advantages in each plan. Accounting helps to show the financial effects of the various options. And there is more to think about than purely financial matters, as you can see.

4 Accounting records and accounts

Earlier on we distinguished between accounting records on the one hand, and accounts (or financial statements) on the other. You may be wondering about the importance of this distinction.

Activity 8

Suppose you help your sister with her market stall business on a Saturday. She keeps a little notebook in which she jots down each transaction as it takes place. She buys her stock from four different suppliers as follows, and pays in cash as noted below:

Supplier A   £100
Supplier B   £250
Supplier C   £50
Supplier D   £175

On Saturday she sells all her goods to ten different customers, noting down the following amounts received in cash: £10, £75, £80, £65, £90, £115, £20, £25, £70, £45, £100.

She also makes a note of paying the market operator £25 cash, and giving you £20 cash for helping her.

Your sister thinks she had a good day. Try to answer this question quickly without using a calculator: did she have a good day?

Unless you have a fantastic head for numbers, you probably couldn't answer this question immediately with any degree of certainty. While your sister's notebook is a form of accounting record for what happened, the numbers don't mean very much listed out separately. What we need is a summary of the different transactions that took place, and this is why we record individual transactions in **accounting records** to produce summary **accounts**.

Using the information from the accounting records that we have been given, we can prepare the following accounts for your sister (for income, stock purchases, stall rent and wages):

Account	Transactions in accounting records £	Total £
Income	10 + 75 + 80 + 65 + 90 + 115 + 20 + 25 + 70 + 45 + 100	695
Expenditure:		
Stock purchases	100 + 250 + 50 + 175	(575)
Stall rent	25	(25)
Wages	20	(20)
Profit for the day		75

(It is an accounting convention to put amounts that are paid out, or owed, in brackets to show that they are to be deducted from the amounts received.)

So she did have a good day!

4.1 Source documents for accounting records

A business of any size can't hope to jot down its transactions in the way that your sister could for one quiet day's trading on her market stall. Also, notice that all your sister's transactions were settled immediately in cash. What if she hadn't paid immediately for her stock, or if she had agreed to wait for payment by one of her customers? How would these transactions be recorded?

Activity 9

5 mins

Your sister's market stall has done well recently and she has now rented premises, acquired a till and opened a business bank account. Some customers come in and pay by cash, but most use cheques, or are themselves businesses and ask for credit (that is, a delay between taking the goods and paying for them). She also persuades a few of her suppliers to allow her credit, so she doesn't have to pay immediately in cash for the stock she buys.

What kinds of document would you expect your sister to be dealing with:

For cash sales? _____

For cash purchases? _____

For sales on credit? _____

For purchases on credit? _____

What documents will your sister be dealing with if customers pay not in cash but by:

Cheque? _____

What documents will she be dealing with if she doesn't pay cash immediately to her suppliers?

_____

What documents will she be dealing with when her credit customers settle their bills?

_____

You may have had to think quite hard about some of these queries, but you could have come up with the following suggestions:

- source documents for cash sales: till roll, receipts to the customers;
- source documents for cash purchases: receipts (again), but from the suppliers for cash received;
- source documents for sales on credit: bills, or sales invoices from your sister to the customers;
- source documents for purchases on credit: bills (again), or invoices from the suppliers to your sister;
- source documents for receipts by cheque: cheques from customers to your sister;
- source documents for payments to credit suppliers: cheques from your sister to her suppliers.

You'll have noticed that I have called these items 'source documents'. This is because they are the source of the information on each transaction that will be recorded in your sister's accounting records, and which will eventually end up summarized in her accounts.

In the case of receipts given to her customers for a cash sale, and sales invoices to her credit customers, the source documents that your sister will keep in her records are copies of what is given away. She will keep the original of the receipt from her supplier for cash received, and of the invoice received from her supplier (often called a purchase invoice, though for the supplier of course it is a sales invoice). For cheques received from her customers she will have to note the details on a paying-in slip before handing the cheques over to her bank. And for cheques to her suppliers she will have to note the details on her cheque stub or counterfoil in her chequebook.

Activity 10

10 mins

Try to find a copy of an invoice from a business that charges Value Added Tax (VAT). You will know that it is an invoice because it must say so by law. What details does it contain?

_____

_____

_____

An invoice with VAT has to contain certain information by law, and contains certain other information by convention. You might have noted down:

- supplier name, address and contact details;
- invoice number;
- customer name and address;
- VAT registration number;
- purchase order number or reference;
- delivery note number or reference;
- **date/tax point**;
- details of the goods or services being invoiced;
- charge for each item;
- rate of VAT applied to each item;
- trade, volume or bulk discount applied;
- **net total of goods/services**;
- **VAT amount**;
- **invoice total (often called the gross total)**;
- credit terms, including the period of credit allowed and whether there are any discounts for early payment;
- remittance advice, for sending back with the payment (often this is a bank giro credit form).

As you can see, there's a lot of information, but I've highlighted the most important information from an invoice that has to be entered in the accounting records.

The other important source document for accounting records is the credit note. Your sister would give one of these to her customer if the customer had returned goods to your sister. Similarly, she would receive a credit note from a supplier to whom she had returned goods.

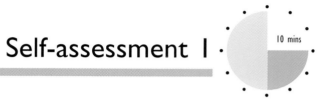

Self-assessment 1

10 mins

1 Complete the following statements by writing a suitable word or words in the space provided.

A company keeps accounting records because it needs to:

a know how much it _____ to other people;

b know how much it is _____ by other people;

c know the value of what it _____ ;

d know what changes need to be made if the money coming into the business is less than the amount _____ to other people;

e be able to _____ for the future.

2 Match each of the following four ways of using money with the **most** appropriate example.

a Medium of exchange.   (i)   Buying a bus ticket.
b Store of wealth.   (ii) An antique clock is valued at £750.
c Means of deferred payment.   (iii) Contributing to a pension plan.
d Measure of value.   (iv) Buying a coat using a credit card.

3 a State how the surplus or profit of an organization is calculated.

_____

_____

b Give **two** reasons why a business needs to make a profit.

_____

_____

4 a Why are source documents important for accounting?

_____

_____

_____

b What is the key information contained in:

I a sales invoice? _____

2 a purchase invoice? _____

3 a cheque? _____

Answers to these questions can be found on page 93.

5 Summary

- The uses of money are as:

  - a medium of exchange;
  - a store of wealth and investment for the future;
  - a means of deferred payment (delayed payment over a period);
  - a common measure of value.

- Organizations keep accounting records to show:

  - how much they owe;
  - how much they are owed;
  - the value of what they own.

- Accounting records enable an organization to monitor day-to-day activities, in order to ensure that expenditure is kept below income. Without this monitoring and control, it would not be possible for the organization to make plans or, in the long term, to survive.

- Accounting principles are used to prepare accounts (or financial statements) from accounting records.

- Source documents, such as receipts for cash paid and received, invoices and cheques, provide key information on the amounts to be recorded for each transaction entered into by an enterprise. Accounting records allow us to record these individual transactions. Accounts are prepared from accounting records and summarise all the individual transactions.

Session B
Finance in business

1 Introduction

You have seen that a business needs to make a profit in order to survive and grow. It also needs start-up money. Where does this money come from? How is it used? How is it controlled so that it can be used at the right time and in the right way?

We constantly hear about the high salaries and salary increases enjoyed by those in charge of very powerful organizations, such as banks. Such salaries are needed to keep the best people at the top and to ensure that the organizations continue to make large profits. Do you agree? Or is ensuring that shareholders are well rewarded the best way for a business to use its profits for the future?

We will aim to answer those questions by the end of this session. You will also see how money can be obtained in different ways and how it is spent to benefit organizations in the short term and longer term. You can also develop your skills so that you will be better able to assess how much of the money generated by businesses is passed on to owners, directors and shareholders, as compared with being reinvested for growth.

We will also look at accounting for cash, which is so necessary to ensure survival.

2 How a business works

2.1 Business capital

Any business needs money to begin. Someone who sets up a cleaning service will need to pay for cleaning materials and, perhaps, advertising. A self-employed editor will need to pay for a computer, modem and printer at the very least. The permanent money used in a business is referred to as **capital** or **capital employed**. In a company, which is a particular legal form for a business, capital is provided in the form of **share capital**; the shares that make up the total share capital are purchased for cash by **shareholders**.

Activity 11

10 mins

George and Mary would like to open a seaside cafe and are wondering what they could use for the opening capital. Which of the following might provide capital? Tick the appropriate box(es).

- Their savings. ☐
- A loan from a bank. ☐
- A gift from an uncle (or other relation). ☐
- Cash from selling a share in the business to someone else. ☐
- George's redundancy money from his last job. ☐

Briefly explain why you might prefer one choice rather than the others.

_____

_____

_____

_____

Any of these sources might be acceptable, although it might be difficult to sell a share in a business that does not yet exist. Setting up in business is risky so George and Mary are likely not to want to use money they might need in the future, or that would involve difficulties with others if the cafe is not successful. So the best choices are probably savings and George's redundancy money, so long as some money remains for them in the event of failure. Providing the gift has 'no strings attached', this may be an even better choice. There would be a legal or moral liability to repay any loan, so if the cafe is unsuccessful George and Mary might not only lose the business but also have to repay the bank or an outsider.

Funds from the owner's own savings and gifts they receive are known as **owner's capital**. Loans, such as from a bank, are called **loan capital**. Accountants might say that a loan is not capital because it needs to be paid back to someone outside the business. They would call it a **creditor**. In practice you will hear both terms used for loans.

2.2 Using capital

If George and Mary use their savings as owner's capital, how would they use it?

Activity 12

Look at the following list of items. Tick those which you think George and Mary might need.

- ■ A building to work from. ☐
- ■ A car or van for distribution. ☐
- ■ Cash till. ☐
- ■ Some form of machinery. ☐

In the space below, write down any other items you think may be needed.

_____

_____

_____

They will need a building for the cafe, which they may buy or rent, cooking equipment, perhaps an ice cream machine, tables and chairs, a cash till and a serving area. A car or van are probably not needed in a business like this. You may have thought of other examples.

> Fixed assets usually stay in an organization for more than a year.

A building, a car or van, equipment and other purchases of this kind will be bought with the intention of keeping them. Under normal circumstances they will not be for re-sale. As such, they are known as **fixed assets**.

Activity 13 · 5 mins

If you start a business and have a building, a car or van, equipment and so on, you can begin work. Or can you? What else does a business need in order to trade? Write down two other things you think you may need.

You may have thought of a number of ideas. Perhaps they included:

- raw materials to be used to make goods with (food, in the case of George and Mary);
- other people to help you in your business;
- fuel, such as electricity.

All these items would have to be paid for. They are the things, and people, that are needed by the business in order to be able to sell goods or services. They are needed day to day and involve the business:

> Current assets and current liabilities are used up in an organization within a year.

- owning things like raw materials, which are part of the **current assets**;
- owing money to people such as employees and the electricity company, called **current liabilities** in accounting (they are also known as creditors);
- being owed money by its customers, known as **debtors**, who are also part of the **current assets**.

Current assets and current liabilities are grouped together and are called **working capital**.

So the owner's capital is used to obtain both the **fixed assets** and to provide the **working capital** (see the diagram, 'How owner's capital is used', below).

Working capital is the money circulating around a company. It flows out when it is used to buy materials and to employ people. It flows back in when goods or services are sold and cash is received.

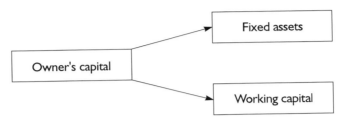

How owner's capital is used

Activity 14

You identified various fixed assets that would be used in George and Mary's cafe. Would the following be current assets or current liabilities? Delete the one you think is incorrect.

- food;   Current asset/Current liability

- the amount owed to the supplier of the food;   Current asset/Current liability

- wages of a waitress;   Current asset/Current liability

- cash in the till.   Current asset/Current liability

All the items are used up within a year and so are current. George and Mary own the food and the cash in the till so these are current assets.

The amounts owed by the business to the supplier and the wages of a waitress are current liabilities.

Let's have a look at another couple of accounting terms you will meet regularly.

- People are often described as any organization's greatest asset. The accounting term for the cost of employing people is **labour**.
- When it is dark and cold you switch on lights and heating. In your business, you would also need to write letters to customers, send out invoices and so on. The costs of electricity, heating and items such as paper and stationery are called **overheads**. If you pay rent to a landlord then the rent is also an overhead.

So the picture of working capital can now be viewed as illustrated in 'Capital and working capital'. The large arrows indicate money flowing into and out of the business. The dotted lines indicate money flowing within the business.

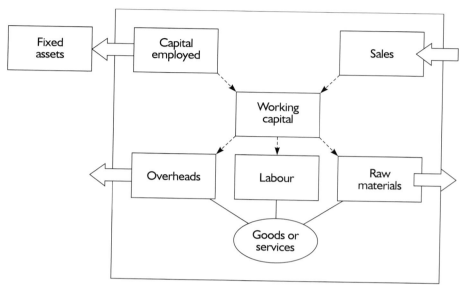

Capital and working capital

Activity 15

In George and Mary's cafe, they would expect to be paid in cash. But Saddiq sells electrical equipment, which is assembled in his factory, to a car manufacturer and sends out an invoice.

What problem might this cause for Saddiq's business?

_____

_____

_____

A delay between the delivery of goods and receipt of payment can cause businesses difficulties and make it difficult for them to pay their bills on time. This problem can put small, and even large, organizations out of business.

It is normal for there to be a delay – a period of credit – between receipt of goods and payment for them. At any one time Saddiq's business will usually be owed money. People who owe money to the business are called its **debtors**. (You may also see these called **accounts receivable**, particularly if you use computer software written outside the UK.)

In turn, the business will owe money to its **creditors**. (These are called **accounts payable** in many places outside the UK.)

Remember the difference between debtors and creditors. They are easy to confuse, but:

EXTENSION 1
If you would like to learn more about computerized accounts, the combination of book and exercise disk listed on page 92 provides a useful introduction.

■ debtors owe money to the business;
■ the business owes money to creditors.

3 Cash flow

To stay in business and make a profit an organization must make sure that cash is available in the right quantity and at the right time to meet its commitments. To understand why this is so important you must get to grips with the fact that profit and cash are different.

When an item is sold for more than it cost to produce the seller makes a profit at the time of the sale. But if the sale is on credit then the profit is not really felt by the seller – or **realized** – until the cash is received from the debtor. During that period of credit the seller may simply run out of cash, so employees can't be paid, debts pile up and the whole thing ends in tears. This explains why so many companies that are 'profitable' fail – they are also, unfortunately, broke.

A cash flow forecast is a statement which identifies expected cash receipts and payments in advance.

Without good control over cash there will be no future in which to try to make a profit. One technique that all businesses use to plan the money flowing in and out of the organization is a **cash flow forecast**. Once a forecast is made, it can then be compared with actual cash receipts and payments, week by week or month by month.

Let's look at an example. The Sharp Bakery has made a cash flow forecast of money coming in and going out of its business. Here is an extract:

Cash flow forecast – weeks 1 to 3				
	Week 1 **£'000**	**Week 2** **£'000**	**Week 3** **£'000**	**Week 4** **£'000**
Cash receipts (sales)				
Bread	150	150	150	
Cakes	250	250	250	
Total cash receipts	400	400	400	
Cash payment				
Ingredients	(106)	(106)	(106)	
Wages	(144)	(144)	(144)	
Overheads	(35)	(35)	(35)	
Van costs	(20)	(20)	(20)	
Total cash payment	(305)	(305)	(305)	
Net cash	95	95	95	
Cash balance B/F	Nil	95	190	
Cash balance C/F	95	190	285	

This statement is a forecast of the flows of cash in the first three weeks of trading of the bakery. Each expected item of cash receipts income is listed and, in this case, this is derived entirely from sales of bread and cakes. Then each expected item of cash payment expenditure is listed. In this case the costs are of making and delivering the bread and cakes.

The difference between receipts (cash in) and payments (cash out) is the forecast cash flow or **balance** or net cash at the end of each week's business. So, to take the first week, £305,000 of cash payments are deducted from £400,000 of cash receipts to give a cash balance of £95,000.

'Balance B/F' means the cash balance brought forward from the previous week and 'Balance C/F' means the cash balance carried forward to the next week. As Week 1 was the first week of business, no cash was brought forward.

Check your understanding of this cash flow statement by completing the next activity.

Activity 16

10 mins

a Looking at the cash flow forecast above, what is the value of the forecast weekly cash sales?

_____

b What is the forecast weekly wage bill?

_____

c What are forecast weekly total cash costs?

_____

d Assuming the figures for cash receipts and payment don't change from week to week, what is the net cash receipt for Week 4?

_____

e Calculate the balance to be carried forward from Week 4 to Week 5.

_____

The correct figures are:

a   £400,000

b   £144,000

c   £305,000

d   £95,000

e   £380,000

We can see the business is forecasting a regular pattern of cash receipts and payments. In a more complicated situation, a business will have to plan for fluctuating receipts and payments.

This forecast can now be used to compare with actual recipts and payments. After the first week's trading, the actual receipts and payments are entered:

	Week 1		Week 2		Week 3		Week 4	
	Forecast £'000	Actual £'000	Forecast £'000	Actual £'000	Forecast £'000	Actual £'000	Forecast £'000	Actual £'000
Receipts								
Bread	150	140	150		150		150	
Cakes	250	220	250		250		250	
Total receipts	400	360	400		400		400	
Payments								
Ingredients	(106)	(112)	(106)		(106)		(106)	
Wages	(144)	(144)	(144)		(144)		(144)	
Overheads	(35)	(35)	(35)		(35)		(35)	
Van costs	(20)	(22)	(20)		(20)		(20)	
Total payments	(305)	(313)	(305)		(305)		(305)	
Net cash	95		95		95		95	
Cash balance B/F	Nil		95		190		285	
Cash balance C/F	95		190		285		380	

Activity 17

5 mins

In the table above, what is the actual cash balance at the end of Week 1?

Write this figure into the cash flow forecast. The actual balance brought forward is nil, so what is the actual balance carried forward to Week 2?

The correct figures are £47,000 at the end of Week 1 and, of course, this is the actual balance carried forward to Week 2. The closing balance of one period is the opening balance of the next.

The amount is calculated by deducting £313,000 from £360,000.

Activity 18 · 5 mins

The second week's actual trading figures for the Sharp Bakery are as follows:

		£'000
Receipts	Bread	150
	Cakes	200
Payments	Ingredients	105
	Wages	144
	Overheads	38
	Van	20

Add these figures to the table opposite and complete the calculation to find out the cash position at the end of week 2, writing it down below.

The cash balance at the end of Week 2 and carried forward for Week 3 is £90,000.

> The comparison of actual figures with forecast ones gives management useful information on which to make decisions.

You can check the cash balance at the end of Week 2 in the table below.

At that stage you can see that the forecast cash balance was £190,000 and the actual position is £100,000 worse than that. You can see that sales have not been as high as expected although the expenditure is not vastly different.

	Week 1 Forecast £'000	Week 1 Actual £'000	Week 2 Forecast £'000	Week 2 Actual £'000	Week 3 Forecast £'000	Week 3 Actual £'000	Week 4 Forecast £'000	Week 4 Actual £'000
Recipts								
Bread	150	140	150	150	150		150	
Cakes	250	220	250	200	250		250	
Total receipts	400	360	400	350	400		400	
Payments								
Ingredients	(106)	(112)	(106)	(105)	(106)		(106)	
Wages	(144)	(144)	(144)	(144)	(144)		(144)	
Overheads	(35)	(35)	(35)	(38)	(35)		(35)	
Van costs	(20)	(22)	(20)	(20)	(20)		(20)	
Total payments	(305)	(313)	(305)	(307)	(305)		(305)	
Net cash	95	47	95	43	95		95	
Cash balance B/F	Nil	Nil	95	47	190		285	
Cash balance C/F	95	47	190	90	285		380	

Now let us take this one step further into weeks 3 and 4.

In Week 3, there is a Bank Holiday. Unfortunately, the bakery had not forecast any change in receipts because of this. During the same week a van crashed and had to be replaced, and an oven also developed a fault. The actual figures for Week 3 were therefore:

Receipts (sales)	Bread	£130,000	
	Cakes	£90,000	
Payments	Ingredients	£106,000	(normal orders for ingredients)
	Wages	£144,000	(Bank Holiday is paid for)
	Overheads	£44,000	(including oven repair)
	Van	£35,000	(including van purchase)

Activity 19 ·

Enter the figures for Week 3 into the cash flow forecast on page 29.

What is the actual cash balance carried forward at the end of Week 3? What does this tell you?

_____

_____

_____

You should have found that the actual cash balance at the end of Week 3 is negative. Receipt of £220,000 less payment of £329,000 gives an outflow of £109,000 cash for the week. And deducting the £109,000 outflow from the opening balance of £90,000 results in a negative balance of £19,000. Therefore, you can see that the amount recorded as the actual balance carried forward for Week 3 in the cash flow forecast below is (£19,000).

This means that the bakery would need to borrow money to cover the excess of payments over receipts or, perhaps, defer payment of some expenditure.

We have also entered figures for Week 4 below. This was a good week:

	Week 1		Week 2		Week 3		Week 4	
	Forecast £'000	Actual £'000	Forecast £'000	Actual £'000	Forecast £'000	Actual £'000	Forecast £'000	Actual £'000
Receipts (sales)								
Bread	150	140	150	150	150	130	150	150
Cakes	250	220	250	200	250	90	250	250
Total receipts	400	360	400	350	400	220	400	400
Payments								
Ingredients	(106)	(112)	(106)	(105)	(106)	(106)	(106)	(100)
Wages	(144)	(144)	(144)	(144)	(144)	(144)	(144)	(144)
Overheads	(35)	(35)	(35)	(38)	(35)	(44)	(35)	(35)
Van costs	(20)	(22)	(20)	(20)	(20)	(35)	(20)	(22)
Total payment	(305)	(313)	(305)	(307)	(305)	(329)	(305)	(301)
Net cash	95	47	95	43	95	(109)	95	99
Cash balance B/F	Nil	Nil	95	47	190	90	285	(19)
Cash balance C/F	95	47	190	90	285	(19)	380	80

Activity 20

5 mins

Now that you have been able to compare actual figures against the forecast ones for the first few weeks, what action, if any, might you consider taking if you were the owner of the bakery?

_____

_____

_____

_____

The bakery has seen that the actual cash flow does not always coincide with its forecasts. As you may agree, the bakery should take note of this, learn to plan a little better, and be careful to keep costs down, especially as they appear to be producing a lot of waste product by producing the same amount of bread and cakes whatever the sales receipts.

EXTENSION 2
Cash flow forecasts are looked at in greater depth in *The Business Plan Workbook*, including their part in a business plan.

In particular, the bakery should remember that sales will be limited in short weeks and should aim not to be over-ambitious in its forecasts.

Activity 21 · 15 mins

S/NVQs B1.1,
D1.1, D1.2

This activity may provide the basis of appropriate evidence for your S/NVQ portfolio. If you are intending to take this course of action, it might be better to write your answers on separate sheets of paper.

Take a look at any cash flow forecast available for your organization or, if that is not possible, you might like to draw one up for a club or society in which you are involved, or even for yourself and your family. Examine the actual results over time against the forecast and prepare a report covering:

■ the success of the forecasting, as compared with actual results;
■ the reasons why there were differences in the actual figures from the forecast (you may need to talk to your manager and others to find out the reasons);
■ what can be learnt from any differences between the forecasting and its results.

Make any recommendations for future cash flow forecasting.

A cash flow forecast is a useful piece of information for management and the above activity will help you appreciate how resources are managed day to day. You may have covered a period where actual results were similar to the cash flow forecast, or discovered that external events can upset plans. You may be faced, as a first line manager, with the need to implement reductions and other changes in operations. Management may have made decisions requiring these actions based on its cash flow forecasting.

Self-assessment 2

1 Match the terms on the left with the descriptions on the right.

a	Owner's capital	(i)	Assets used within the business, and not intended for resale.
b	Fixed assets	(ii)	Capital provided by the business owner.
c	Working capital	(iii)	People the business owes money to.
d	Labour	(iv)	People who owe the business money.
e	Overheads	(v)	Current assets less current liabilities.
f	Debtors	(vi)	The cost to the business of its employees.
g	Creditors	(vii)	The incidental expenses incurred in running a business, including fuel and rent.

2 In the first two months of operation, Julia Ferguson had the following transactions:

May
- Opening capital £450
- Receipts from sales £1,040
- Materials paid for £500
- Overheads £200

June
- Receipt from sales £990
- Materials paid for £560
- Overheads £210

When she started her business, Julia hoped to be able to purchase a second-hand delivery van for £1,000 at the start of July.

Identify and explain whether or not this is possible.

3 Briefly explain the problems that are likely to arise when a business decides to offer customers a six month interest free credit period after previously allowing customers only one month credit.
What are the benefits of making an offer like this?

Answers to these questions can be found on pages 94–5.

4 Summary

- Capital comes from:

  - the owners, when it is known as owners' capital;
  - issuing shares to other people, when it is known as share capital;
  - loans, when it is known as loan capital. Loans have to be paid back and are also known as creditors.

- Capital is:

  - invested in fixed assets, such as buildings, which are not normally for resale;
  - used as working capital which circulates in the business and is used to produce eventual sales of goods or services. Working capital comprises raw materials and other current assets as well as current liabilities.

- Debtors owe money to the business, while creditors are owed money by the business.

- Overheads are the general expenses of running a business, for example heat, light, rent and telephone.

- A cash flow forecast is a way of planning, monitoring and controlling what is likely to happen in the coming period so far as receipts and payments are concerned. Even a forecast that proves to be somewhat inaccurate can be used to anticipate problems and plan for expected shortages.

Session C
Financial information

1 Introduction

In this session we will look at the way accounting procedures are used in organizations to prepare the year-end financial statements, such as the published annual reports and accounts of companies.

These annual reports represent an organization's effort to the outside world and provide useful information for shareholders, potential investors, lenders, employees and others.

Because of the importance given to financial information by influential contacts of businesses, these financial statements are very important and your studies in this session will improve your ability to read and understand them.

Certainly it is questionable how many people actually understand financial statements. Clear signs of problems are often in the accounts of companies, such as Enron, which hit the headlines with their failures. Perhaps people find them too boring or complicated to read, or are too trusting. You would think that if their job was on the line, or if they risked losing several thousand or million of pounds, they would be more interested, wouldn't you?

How much of your pension fund is invested in companies quoted on the London Stock Exchange? How much do you know about them? Do you want to know more?

First of all, we need to look at the very significant effect of the fact we saw above – that not all the transactions entered into by businesses are settled immediately in cash.

2 Cash accounting versus profit accounting

We saw above that the cash flow forecast looks at transactions in terms of cash flow. In each month, a business assesses how much it will pay out as cash and how much it will receive in. This means that it can plan to have enough of its lifeblood, cash, to survive and grow.

Activity 22 · 10 mins

Johnson Ltd makes sales of £10,000 in its first month of trading, November, and incurs expenses of £6,500. Only 50% of its customers settle their bills in November, and Johnson Ltd pays only 10% of its expenses in the month.

By how much do Johnson Ltd's cash receipts exceed its cash payments for November?

_____

_____

By how much does Johnson Ltd's income (sales) exceed its expenses in November? What is this figure usually called?

_____

_____

Explain why the two figures you have calculated are different.

_____

_____

You should have calculated that Johnson Ltd received cash of £5,000 (£10,000 × 50%) in November, and paid out only £650 (£6,500 × 10%). In cash terms, therefore, its receipts exceeded its payments by £4,350. But Johnson Ltd sold only £3,500 more than it incurred as expenses in November (£10,000–£6,500). The figure of £3,500 is its profit for November.

Don't worry if you struggled a little to explain the difference. It comes from the fact that the figure of £3,500 is calculated by taking into account *both* sales and purchases that have been settled in cash *and* those that have not. If Johnson Ltd made no transactions in December, but simply waited for the cash to roll in while paying its bills, by the end of December it would have received only £3,500 more than it paid out, as all the November transactions would have been realized in cash. The fact that its receipts and payments situation looks better than its income and expenses position at the end of November is purely down to the fact that Johnson Ltd is better at getting money in from its debtors than it is at paying its creditors.

Looking at income and expenses, whether realized or unrealized in the form of cash, is called **profit (or accruals) accounting**, and is the principle that underlies the financial information that we will examine in the rest of this session.

3 The profit and loss account

You have seen that by making up a cash flow forecast for the *future* on the basis of likely receipts and payments, and monitoring it weekly or monthly, a business has a way of planning and controlling its lifeblood, which is the availability of cash.

An organization measures its *past* operations through a **profit and loss account**. This is a summary of a company's financial performance over the last year, rather than how it is likely to operate in the future.

A profit and loss account shows what a business has earned in total, known as **income** or **revenue**, against what it has spent, known as **expenses**. Where revenue exceeds expenses, the business has made a **profit**. Where expenses exceed income, the business has made a **loss**.

A simplified profit and loss account might look like this:

Hillside Company Limited

Profit and loss account for the year ended 31 March

	£	£
Sales		100,000
Less cost of goods sold		(40,000)
Gross profit		60,000
Labour	20,000	
Overheads	20,000	(40,000)
Net profit for the year		£20,000

The right-hand column shows how expenses (in brackets) are deducted from income, and the resulting profit figures. The centre, numerical, column shows how sub-totals are made up.

Two important features in the account are as follows:

■ **Gross profit:** this measures the company's success at buying and selling goods or services. The part of the financial statement in which gross profit is calculated is often called the **trading account**.

■ **Net profit:** this measures the success of the company's operations for the year. The costs of wages and salaries and other overheads are deducted from the gross profit to arrive at the net profit.

There are several important differences between the two types of accounting we have looked at so far (profit accounting and cash accounts), and they affect the profit and loss account. The main ones are listed in the table below:

	Profit accounting	**Cash accounting**
Sales	As long as invoices have been sent out, a profit and loss account recognizes them as money coming in even before the cash has been received.	Cash is only recognized when it has been received.
Fixed assets	When a fixed asset is sold, it is the profit or loss on the sale which is accounted for – that is, the cash received from the cost of the fixed asset.	When a fixed asset is sold, the total cash value of the sale is accounted for – the cash available.
Expenses	Invoices that have been received, and even goods or services that have been received but without an invoice, are recognized as money going out even before the cash has been paid.	What is recognized is what is actually paid.

3.1 Cost of goods sold

Trading businesses buy goods at one price, put them in stock and later hope to sell them at a higher price. To find out how much stock they have at the end of one financial year, they carry out stocktaking. Stocktaking is done to arrive at the true stock position at the end of a trading year, known as the **closing stock**. This will also be the value of stock for the beginning of the next year, and therefore is referred to as the **opening stock** for that year.

Some organizations have end-of-year stocktaking where all the stock is counted. Others use perpetual stocktaking where continual records, on computer, are kept and checks on stock are made throughout the year.

In the case of the Hillside Company, the end of the financial year is March. The figure for the cost of goods sold was found by taking the opening stock figure, adding materials purchased during the year (whether paid for or not), and taking away the closing stock figure:

	£
Opening stock	10,000
Add purchases	50,000
Less closing stock	(20,000)
Cost of goods sold	40,000

Activity 23

10 mins

Here are the figures for a year's trading to 31 March for Straton Limited, calculated on a profit accounting basis (that is, ignoring whether or not sales or expenses have been settled in cash).

	£
Sales	60,000
Opening stock	10,000
Purchases	20,000
Closing stock	5,000
Overheads	10,000
Wages	15,000

Produce a profit and loss account for Straton Limited. What are the gross and net profits?

_____

_____

_____

_____

_____

_____

_____

_____

_____

_____

_____

_____

_____

_____

_____

_____

_____

The answer to this activity can be found on page 97.

3.2 Deductions from profit

The profit and loss accounts we have looked at so far have been simplified ones. There are other expenses in a business which must be taken into account.

Activity 24 · 5 mins

Think about other expenses that your organization has in relation to its fixed assets, and write down **two** below:

_____

_____

You may have mentioned such expenses as insurance, repairs and running costs. An important item you may not have included in your list is **depreciation**.

Depreciation is a feature of profit accounting that does not appear as such in cash accounts. This is because it is a way of charging the cost of a fixed asset to the profit and loss account, reducing profit over a period of some years.

Say Barnard Ltd bought a large mechanical digger for £50,000 and paid for it in cash. It planned to use the digger in its business for twenty years.

In cash accounting, this fixed asset purchase would appear as an increase in payments of £50,000 in the year it was paid for. In profit accounting, however, the digger would be depreciated, so that each year of its useful life receives some charge for the fixed asset. Depreciation might be in equal instalments over the twenty years of its useful life, so each year – even the year it was bought – receives the same charge of £50,000/20 = £2,500. Or it might be by some other method, which makes a higher charge in earlier years when the digger is more effective.

You can see that charging depreciation over a period, rather than the full cost at one time will make a great deal of difference to a company's apparent profitability. Remember, though, that the cash is still gone. **Depreciation does not affect cash flow; fixed asset purchases do.**

Other 'deductions' you will see in a company profit and loss account include:

- tax against profits levied by government, such as corporation tax;
- dividends to be paid to shareholders.

Shareholders, who invest in a company by buying shares, are part owners of the company. If the business does badly, they may lose their money. They therefore expect a reward from the business when it does well, to compensate for the risk they are taking.

Dividends are seen as ways of sharing out the profit earned, known as **appropriations of profit**.

Let's continue the profit and loss account for Straton Limited using some slightly different terms.

Straton Limited
Profit and loss account for the year ended 31 March

	£	£
Turnover		60,000
Cost of sales		(25,000)
Gross profit		35,000
Operating expenses		
Wages	(15,000)	
Overheads	(10,000)	
Rates	(2,000)	
Interest on loan	(2,000)	
Depreciation	(3,000)	(32,000)
Profit on ordinary activities before taxation		3,000
Tax on profit on ordinary activities		(400)
Profit on ordinary activities after taxation		2,600
Dividends paid		(1,000)
Retained profit		1,600

This is the sort of structure or layout you will see in your own or another company's annual report and accounts, although you may notice some differences. For example, other items may be shown. Note that in the above **turnover** is another name for sales, and **profit on ordinary activities before taxation** is the same as net profit.

The profit figure before tax is usually called the **pre-tax profit**. The **retained profit** is the final surplus which a business can use to reinvest in itself for growth.

3.2 Income and expenditure accounts

So far the examples we've looked at have concentrated on businesses of various sizes, that are aiming to make a profit. What accounting principles hold true for non-profit organizations? They don't aim to make a profit, so is profit accounting appropriate?

In fact the same accounting principles hold true for non-profit organizations as for profit making ones, so profit accounting is appropriate. The reason is this: if accounts only showed cash transactions (actual receipts and payments) then an organization could easily manipulate its figures at a particular year end simply by not paying its bills until after the year end. Nobody reading the financial statements would know about the unpaid liabilities. This would not be a good way for any organization, a business or a non-profit one such as a club, a society, a charity or a public sector body, to present its affairs.

There are some differences of terminology, however. A non-profit organization presents an **income and expenditure account**, rather than a profit and loss account. Instead of a profit it might report a **surplus of income over expenditure**; instead of a loss there might be a **deficit**, or an **excess of expenditure over income**.

There are also considerable differences in operations.

Activity 25 · 15 mins

Take a look at the end-of-year financial statements of your own organization and two or three others, say, a bank or building society, a club or a charity.

Look at the profit and loss accounts or income and expenditure accounts. Note down, on a separate sheet of paper, the various names used for:

- sales or turnover;
- gross profit;
- net profit;
- retained profit.

You now have a greater understanding of the terminology used in different organizations and, in particular, your own. This will help you in understanding how resources have been used and the financial results of their use. You may have seen **fees**, donations, grants, subscriptions or **takings** for sales or turnover; **trading profit** for gross profit; **surplus of income over expenditure** for net profit; **undistributed profit** or **undistributed surplus** for retained profit, and so on.

Whilst looking for the specific features of profit and loss statements and income and expenditure accounts, you probably saw a number of different terms used for types of expenditure which represent the use of resources. If you have extra time to study these, this will improve your overall understanding of financial information.

4 The balance sheet

The **balance sheet** is a 'snapshot' of a company's assets and liabilities at a specific moment in time, say 31 May, which tells us where the money is used and where it came from.

One difference between a balance sheet and a profit and loss account (or income and expenditure account) is that the latter is a statement of what has happened over a period of time – usually a year.

Before moving on let's remind ourselves about some terms we have already met.

Activity 26 · 5 mins

Complete the following statements.

1 If someone owes us money they are _____.

2 If we owe money to someone, they are _____.

3 A fixed asset is something owned which _____

_____.

4 Give two examples of a fixed asset: _____

and _____.

This is a revision of your earlier work; if you had any difficulties, you should refer back and check your previous studies.

1 If someone owes us money they are DEBTORS.

2 If we owe money to someone, they are CREDITORS.

3 A fixed asset is something owned which is normally not for sale.

4 Examples of fixed assets are: a car; a computer bought for use in the business; machinery; a building; ... anything purchased for use in an enterprise over a period longer than a year.

4.1 Assets and liabilities

To know how you stand financially you need to list what you **owe**, what is **owed to you** and what you **own**. In businesses the same applies and we use terms such as **assets** and **liabilities** in our lists.

A personal computer, an article produced in the factory for sale, cash in the bank, or money owed by a customer are all of value to a business, because they can be used by the business or will bring money into the business.

Assets are things that are of value to a business.

Other things dealt with in financial accounts, such as money owed to a supplier, or business rates owed to the council, represent claims against the business.

Claims against a business are called liabilities.

Activity 27

5 mins

Look at each of these items and decide whether it is an ASSET or a LIABILITY. Delete the one you think is incorrect.

a Debtors.   ASSET/~~LIABILITY~~
b Creditors.   ~~ASSET~~/LIABILITY
c Cash in the bank. ASSET/~~LIABILITY~~
d Buildings.   ASSET/~~LIABILITY~~
e Machinery.   ASSET/~~LIABILITY~~
f Vehicles.   ASSET/~~LIABILITY~~
g Goods for sale.   ASSET/~~LIABILITY~~
h Corporation tax. ~~ASSET~~/LIABILITY
i Overdraft.   ~~ASSET~~/LIABILITY

The ASSETS in the list are:

a   Debtors (people who owe us money).
c   Cash in the bank.
d   Buildings.
e   Machinery.
f   Vehicles.
g   Goods for sale.

There are three LIABILITIES:

b   Creditors (people we owe money to).
h   Corporation tax.
i   Overdraft.

Earlier in this workbook we talked briefly about current and fixed assets. You will remember that fixed assets are worth money and will not normally be sold or converted into cash. The assets that are already cash, such as cash in the bank, or that are going to be turned into cash very quickly, like debtors, are current assets.

Activity 28 · 5 mins

Tick which of the following assets are fixed assets.

a   Debtors.   ☐
b   Cash in the bank.   ☐
c   Buildings.   ☐
d   Machinery.   ☐
e   Vehicles.   ☐
f   Goods for sale.   ☐

Fixed assets are held for the longer term and include:

c   Buildings.
d   Machinery.
e   Vehicles.

The other assets – debtors, cash in the bank and goods for sale – are all **current assets**.

You will also see **current liabilities** in the accounts of organizations. Typical examples are trade creditors (suppliers), a bank overdraft and, in a company, the tax and dividends owing. Tax is a private matter for a sole trader or partners.

There are also **long-term liabilities**. These are claims against the business such as:

- loans from a bank or elsewhere that are repayable in more than a year;

- amounts owed under leases.

We saw earlier that **owner's capital** is a kind of long-term liability. This is because these funds will eventually, in theory, have to be repaid to the owners, just like a bank loan will have to be repaid. And just as the bank accepts interest as the 'price' of the loan over time, owners seek some sort of return on the capital they have provided.

For sole traders and partners, the return they receive is called **drawings** (literally, they draw money out of the business). Shareholders in a company receive **dividends** as their return on capital. (The fact that shareholders in companies that are listed on a stock exchange can make a profit individually, by selling their shares at a higher price than they bought them for, is basically a bonus that has little or nothing to do with the company.)

Sometimes you will hear the term '**equity**' used in the context of company shareholders. All this means is that each shareholder of, say, a £1 share has an equal right to receive a return on that £1 share as any other shareholder of a £1 share.

4.2 Preparing a balance sheet

At least once a year, and often more frequently, the assets and liabilities of a business are listed in a statement called a **balance sheet**.

A simple, but incomplete, balance sheet may look like this (eventually the totals on the left and the right sides will be the same, or 'balance'):

Jute Jewels Limited

Balance sheet as at 31 March

	£	£		£
Fixed assets				
Buildings	4000			
Machinery	800		(we will put an	
Vehicles	1,000		entry in this	
		5,800	section shortly)	
Current assets			*Current liabilities*	
Stock	1,000		Creditors	500
Debtors	1,000			
Cash at bank	500	2,500		
		£8,300		£500

This balance sheet is incomplete. It is easy to tell this fact, because it doesn't yet balance – the two sides are not equal. Every balance sheet must show that the total assets equal the total liabilities plus capital.

If we deduct the immediate claims against the business (the current liabilities) from the things that are of value to the business (the assets) in this balance sheet, we are left with £7,800, which is called the **capital employed** in the business.

Capital employed is total assets less current liabilities.

Depending on the type of business, capital employed can comprise:

■ long-term liabilities – bank loans, leases, debentures (long-term loans to bodies other than banks);
■ owner's capital.

We can now complete the balance sheet:

Jute Jewels Limited				
Balance sheet as at 31 March				
	£	£		£
Fixed assets			Capital	7,800
Buildings	4,000			
Machinery	800			
Vehicles	1,000			
		5,800		
Current assets			*Current liabilities*	
Stock	1,000		Creditors	500
Debtors	1,000			
Cash at bank	500	2,500		
		£8,300		£8,300

Now you can see why it is called a balance sheet: the **total assets balance the total liabilities**.

Activity 29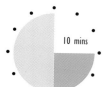

10 mins

Decide which of the following are assets and which are liabilities. Then enter them as appropriate in the balance sheet below. Calculate the capital employed (total assets minus current liabilities) and enter the figure in the right place on the balance sheet.

Hint

Debtors	10,000	There are:
Creditors	12,000	
Cash at bank	800	three fixed assets
Factory	50,000	three current assets
Machinery	8,000	one current liability
Vehicles	1,000	
Goods for sale	3,000	

Balance sheet as at 31 December

£   £   £

Fixed assets   Capital

Current assets   Current liabilities

Let's see how you did. You should have added up the total assets and subtracted the creditors to arrive at capital. Did you?

Balance sheet as at 31 December					
	£	£			£
Fixed assets			Capital		60,800
Factory	50,000		(balancing figure)		
Vehicles	1,000				
Machinery	8,000	59,000			
Current assets			*Current liabilities*		
Goods for sale	3,000		Creditors		12,000
Debtors	10,000				
Cash at bank	800	13,800			
		£72,800			£72,800

You'll notice that the total of the assets side of the balance sheet is the same as the total of the liabilities side.

A balance sheet does not tell us what a business is worth. Instead, it tells us how the business is financed.

In the previous activity, for example, the business is made up of three different fixed assets and three different current assets. These assets are financed by £60,800 worth of capital and £12,000 worth of credit at the time the balance sheet is drawn up.

4.3 The balance sheet and the profit and loss account

You may be wondering why – if the balance sheet is a snapshot and the profit and loss account (or, indeed, the income and expenditure account) covers a period of a year or so – the two statements are always presented together.

The reason is that the two parts are very closely linked, namely by the capital section in the balance sheet, to the retained profit in the profit and loss account.

Basically the retained profit for the period (shown in the profit and loss account) is added to the owner's capital (shown in the previous balance sheet) to arrive at the new balance sheet. The fact that the enterprise has made money, be it a profit or a surplus, in the period causes the total assets less current liabilities – often called the net assets – to increase. In turn this means there is an increase in the capital section.

See for yourself, by completing the activity below. Note the slightly different layout of the balance sheet, which separates capital employed completely from total assets less current liabilities, or **net assets**. The vertical format is also a common presentation. Finally, the accumulated retained profit over years is usually referred to as the **profit and loss reserve**.

Activity 30

15 mins

At 1 January the balance sheet of Crombie Ltd was as follows:

Crombie Ltd	
Balance sheet as at 1 January	
	£
Total assets	100,000
Current liabilities	(30,000)
Net assets	70,000
Share capital	20,000
Total profit retained in previous years (profit and loss reserve)	50,000
Capital employed	70,000

By 31 December Crombie Ltd had generated a retained profit for the year, as shown in its profit and loss account, of £15,000. Total assets had increased by £35,000, and current liabilities by £20,000.

Fill in the spaces in the balance sheet below.

Crombie Ltd
Balance sheet as at 31 December

	£
Total assets	
Current liabilities	_____
Net assets	_____
Share capital	20,000
Profit and loss reserve	50,000
Retained profit for the year	_____
Capital employed	_____

Did your balance sheet balance? Simply by adding the figures given to those in the brought forward balance sheet, you should have come up with the following balance sheet.

Crombie Ltd
Balance sheet as at 31 December

	£
Total assets	135,000
Current liabilities	(50,000)
Net assets	85,000
Share capital	20,000
Profit and loss reserve	50,000
Retained profit for the year	15,000
Capital employed	85,000

Before we leave this topic, consider briefly how Crombie Ltd's balance sheet would be affected if its shareholders had introduced £5,000 cash into the business (in return for shares).

The effect of this would simply be to increase net assets by £5,000 and to increase share capital by £5,000. The balance sheet totals would be £90,000 instead of £85,000.

However complicated a set of financial statements may look on the surface – and they can look very complicated indeed – you have now covered the basic principles which underlie their purpose and their preparation.

4.4 The balance sheet and the income and expenditure account

We need one last word on non-profit organizations. You will remember that an income and expenditure account will show a surplus of income over expenditure, or a deficit. Where does this appear on the organization's balance sheet?

The capital section of a non-profit organization's balance sheet is where it differs from those for businesses. These organizations have assets and liabilities just like a business, but instead of share capital or owner's capital, they have **funds or reserves**. There is a lot of variety in the terminology used for these funds, depending on the type of organization and its history. Below are some examples:

- founder's fund;
- endowment fund;
- building fund;
- bursary reserve;
- life fund;
- accumulated fund or reserve.

You may have found others when you looked at examples in earlier activities.

Some of these funds might be of a fixed amount, say where the founders of a charity gave it a fixed amount as its *founder's fund*. Some may be permanent in nature but can increase when certain payments are received by the organization, such as an *endowment fund* or a *bursary reserve*. Some may be set up with a particular objective in mind and be increased with surpluses and reduced with deficits until the objective is fulfilled, such as a *building fund*. Some may be required by the organization's constitution or by law, as a way of showing the amount of specific inflows of cash to the organization over time, such as a *life fund* in a life insurer. And some may simply be the equivalent of the profit and loss reserve in a business – the accumulated reserve.

Activity 31 ·

30 mins

S/NVQ DI.I

This activity may provide the basis of appropriate evidence for your S/NVQ portfolio. If you are intending to take this course of action, it might be better to write your answers on separate sheets of paper.

Take a look at the year-end financial statements of your own organization and two or three others, say, a bank or building society, a club or charity.

Look at the balance sheets of each and make a list of the different kinds of fixed and current assets, current and long-term liabilities and capital financing that you find.

This will add to your understanding of the terminology used in different organizations. The assets indicate the resources owned by each organization, and the liabilities and capital show how those resources have been financed. If you looked at the balance sheet of a financial organization you will have seen that the balance sheet concentrates on loans, advances and deposits and differs strongly from other balance sheets.

You should now have a good idea of the different financial data you can expect to meet and how they are presented.

Now look at your own role.

■ What specific fixed and current assets do you and your team use? What is the approximate value of the assets you use and what fraction of the organization's total assets does this amount to?

■ Could you do anything to improve the way that you use these assets to benefit the organization, or reduce its liabilities (e.g. by reducing its need to borrow money)?

Self-assessment 3 ·

20 mins

I Draw up a profit and loss account for Lester Limited using the following information. The company trading year ends on 31 December. Use the framework provided. (All figures are in £'000.)

a Cash sales were £352.
b Credit sales were £400.
c Stock at the beginning of the year was valued at £20.
d Stock at the end of the year was valued at £70.
e Purchases during the year came to £520.

752

(520 – 50)

f   Operating expenses, apart from stock, came to £120.
g   The company paid interest of £12 on loans.
h   Depreciation was calculated at £40.
i   Taxation is at a rate of 20% on profit.
j   The dividend was £4.

> ### Lester Limited
> ### Profit and Loss Account for the year ended 31st December
>
> | | £'000 | £'000 |
> |---|---|---|
> | Sales | | |
> | Cost of goods sold | | |
> | Gross profit | | |
> | *Overhead expenses* | | |
> | | | |
> | | | |
> | Profit before tax | | |
> | Tax | | |
> | Profit after tax | | |
> | Dividend | | |
> | Retained profit | | |

2   Complete the following statements with a suitable word.

  a   Assets that are to be kept and used in the business are _____ assets.

  b   Assets that are expected to be turned into cash very soon are _____ assets.

  Why is it important to identify the difference between types of asset?

  _____

  _____

  _____

  _____

3   Match the following items with their descriptions.

  a Working capital.   (i)   Statement in which assets equal liabilities.
  b Capital employed.   (ii) Current assets less current liabilities.
  c Depreciation.   (iii) Amount written off the value of a fixed asset.
  d Balance sheet.   (iv) Long-term liabilities and owner's funds.

Answers to these questions can be found on page 95–6.

5 Summary

- A profit and loss account measures financial performance over a defined period. From it you can learn what a business has earned (revenue) and what it has spent (operating expenses).

- To arrive at profit before tax, all operating expenses, including interest paid on loans and depreciation, must be included.

- The retained profit is obtained after dividends have been paid to shareholders, if it is for a company. The figure is transferred to the balance sheet and is the surplus money that is re-invested in the business.

- Money and anything that can be turned into money are **assets**.

- Claims against the company are **liabilities**.

- Assets are either:

  - current: they are (or could be) turned into cash fairly quickly;
  - fixed: they are kept and used by the business rather than being turned into cash.

- A balance sheet is a snapshot at a particular time of the business' assets and liabilities balanced against each other. It shows what a business owns (assets) balanced by how these assets are financed (liabilities).

- Non-profit organizations prepare income and expenditure accounts, which are very similar to profit and loss accounts. A surplus is transferred to the accumulated fund in the organization's balance sheet, or to some other specific fund or reserve.

Session D
Financial indicators

1 Introduction

You have seen that a great deal of information is available from financial statements. However, you may wonder how this information can be used.

One answer is that it can be used to analyse companies to discover how healthy they are. In this session, we will look at a few important ratios, that is, measures or indicators of the performance of a business.

Whenever a bank is approached for a loan, or a pension fund is considering investing in the Stock Exchange, they will calculate a number of ratios to give them an idea about the performance of the organizations which are potentially going to get their money. Analysis by ratios helps them estimate the risks they will be taking.

You and your workteam, the human assets of a company, do not appear in a balance sheet, either as assets or liabilities! However, you bring your skills, knowledge and experience to work and are key to a company's performance. Almost every part of an organization contributes to the control of current assets and minimizing of current liabilities, whether you are in planning, production, marketing, stock control, credit control or whatever. So, financial indicators are a measure of you, your team, and your management's performance.

Financial indicators can be calculated for a business as a whole, using positioned financial statements, or for parts of it. The latter approach means that the performance of individual managers can be measured.

2 Using ratio analysis

A ratio is a relationship between one number and another. If one workteam has twelve people and another has eight people, the ratio of their numbers could be expressed in any of the following ways:

as 12:8   *or as* $\dfrac{12}{8}$ *or as* 3:2   *or as* $\dfrac{3}{2}$ *or as* 1.5:1   *or as* 1.5 to 1

Financial indicators are usually presented in one of the last two forms in the list above.

We shall look at some key financial measures of business performance, discussing liquidity (the ability to pay debts) and profitability.

2.1 Current ratios (liquidity)

You will remember that current assets are cash or nearly cash. Current liabilities are debts which have to be paid soon. A wise business will have enough current assets to ensure that they can pay current liabilities.

The main reason for business failure is the inability to pay debts when due, because of lack of liquid cash. Such a business is **insolvent**.

This idea gives us an important ratio or test called the **current ratio**:

$$\text{Current ratio} = \frac{\text{Current assets}}{\text{Current liabilities}}$$

If we want to know if a business is **solvent**, that is whether it can cover its debts, we would calculate the current ratio.

The current ratio is also called the **working capital ratio** because it compares the different aspects of working capital: current assets and current liabilities.

Activity 32 · 5 mins

In the balance sheet for Lee Lay Chin, the current assets are £13,800 and the current liabilities are £12,000.

■ What is her current ratio?

_____

_____

_____

■ Do you think her business is solvent?

_____

_____

_____

_____

The current ratio is $\dfrac{£13,800}{£12,000}$ = 1.15 to 1, so the business is solvent. A ratio of 1:1 or higher would mean it had enough current assets to pay all its immediate liabilities.

What we cannot guarantee, of course, is that the current assets, such as stock and debtors, can be turned into cash quickly enough to pay off the current liabilities when they are due. Customers supplied with goods and services on credit tend to take a month to pay generally, and stocks are likely to take even longer to turn into cash. If a business generally sells goods on credit, it will first need to sell the goods and then collect from the debtors who buy the goods before seeing the cash.

Therefore, we have a sharper test of solvency called the **quick ratio** or **'acid test'**. We take away stock from current assets and that gives us the **quick assets**. These are the assets which can be turned into cash quickly or are cash already.

$$\text{Acid test} = \dfrac{\text{Current assets} - \text{Stock}}{\text{Current liabilities}}$$

Activity 33 ·

Assume that Lee Lay Chin has stock valued at £3,000 in her current assets. What is her quick ratio?

_____

_____

_____

Here, the calculations are:

$$\text{Quick ratio} = \frac{£13,800 - £3,000}{£12,000} = 0.9:1$$

This would still be considered as a healthy position – but only just! If you read textbooks on this subject, you are likely to see that recommended levels for these ratios are:

- current ratio 2:1;
- quick ratio 1:1.

But much depends on the type of business. A supermarket turns its stock into cash very quickly and will usually have money available to pay its debts. It can survive on much lower ratios than, say, a manufacturer of luxury yachts who would have plenty of cash each time a yacht was sold, but would be building up stock for most of the time as each yacht is put together. To be truly solvent a yacht manufacturer might need a current ratio of 4:1, 5:1 or more.

The best way to check solvency is to use both these ratios and a cash flow forecast (which we looked at in Session B) so you would get a good view of how the cash is flowing through the organization to meet liabilities.

To use ratio analysis properly, an accountant would:

Various books are available listing ratios for different industries and sizes of business.

- compare an organization's ratios with those of other organizations in the same line of business;
- compare the ratios with a known standard for an industry, if there is one.

2.2 Profit margin (profitability)

You might want to look at the profitability of sales in your business. This is called the profit margin and indicates what return a business is making as a result of its efforts.

For this we go to the profit and loss account and look at profit in relation to sales (revenue or turnover).

This indicator or ratio is expressed as a percentage (%):

$$\text{Profit margin} = \frac{\text{Profit before tax}}{\text{Sales revenue}} \times 100$$

Profit margin is also known as the **net profit percentage**.

Activity 34

5 mins

In the profit and loss account of Straton Limited which you saw earlier, the pre-tax profit was £3,000 and sales revenue was £60,000. What is the profit margin?

_____

_____

_____

_____

The profit margin of Straton Limited is:

$$\frac{£3,000}{£60,000} \times 100 = 5\%$$

So, for every £1 of sales, the company made 5p net profit.

Again, to make sense of this indicator you would need to compare this with earlier results of the company and with the typical results for the industry. It is this comparison with the past, with other organizations, and with industry standards, which makes ratio analysis useful.

Activity 35

5 mins

Here are two consecutive years' results for Network Ltd and Bryn Ltd.

In year 1, Network Ltd has
  sales of   £100,000
  pre-tax profits of   £7,000

In year 2, it has
  sales of   £120,000
  pre-tax profits of   £8,000

In year 1, Bryn Ltd has
  sales of   £400,000
  pre-tax profits of   £23,000

In year 2, it has
  sales of   £380,000
  pre-tax profits of   £22,000

1 What is the profit margin of Network Ltd for each year?

_____

_____

_____

2 What is the profit margin of Bryn Ltd for each year?

_____

_____

_____

3 Which of the companies has improved its profit margin?

_____

_____

1 Network Ltd's profit margin is:

$$\frac{\text{Profit before tax}}{\text{Sales revenue}} \times 100 = \frac{7}{100} \times 100 = 7\% \text{ in Year 1}$$

and

$$\frac{8}{120} \times 100 = 6.67\% \text{ in Year 2}$$

2 Using the same formula, Bryn Ltd's profit margin is 5.75% in Year 1, and 5.79% in Year 2.

3 Bryn Ltd has improved its profit margin while that of Network Ltd has fallen.

2.3 Return on capital (profitability)

If you were thinking about investing in another business you would be interested in the **return on capital employed (ROCE)**. This shows how well the business uses the money invested in it.

The ROCE ratio is expressed as a percentage (%):

$$\text{Return on capital employed} = \frac{\text{Profit before tax}}{\text{Capital employed}} \times 100$$

Pre-tax profit is the same as the profit figure you used for the profit margin and comes from the profit and loss account. Capital employed is obtained from the balance sheet. It is calculated as capital plus reserves, or you will get the same figure by taking away current and long-term liabilities from total assets.

Activity 36

5 mins

The capital employed in The Orange Company Ltd is £860,000. Its pre-tax profit is £65,000. What is the return on capital employed for the company?

_____

_____

_____

The ROCE (figures in £'000) is:

$$\frac{£65}{£860} \times 100 = 7.56\%$$

EXTENSION 3
If you would like to look
at financial indicators in
greater depth, take a
look at *Business
Accounting* by Alan
Sangster and Frank
Wood.

As with other ratios, the typical return on capital employed for a particular industry may differ widely from the ROCE in another industry. Generally, ratios relating to profits and returns reflect the risks in different organizations. An investor would expect a higher profit margin and return to compensate for the risk of losing everything.

Activity 37

S/NVQs B1.2, D1.1, D1.2

This activity may provide the basis of appropriate evidence for your S/NVQ portfolio. If you are intending to take this course of action, it might be better to write your answers on separate sheets of paper.

Take a look at the year-end financial statements of your own organization and two or three others, say, a bank or building society, a club or charity, which you obtained earlier.

- Calculate the current and quick ratios, the profit margin and the return on capital employed for each. If the financial statements give figures for the previous year as well, as is common, calculate ratios for that year too.
- What does this tell you about the organization's performance?
- In what way might the performance of your own workteam have contributed to any changes in performance?
- What steps might you take to improve the organization's performance, or to sustain past improvements?

Prepare a report comparing the results of the different organizations, and for the same organization over the last two years if you have figures available.

The ratios you have calculated assist in measuring the business performance of organizations and show how well resources have been used. Your report is typical of the analysis which management and others perform regularly.

Self-assessment 4

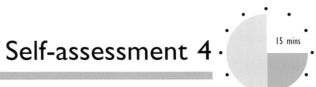

15 mins

1   What is the current ratio of a charity with current assets of £240,000 and current liabilities of £400,000?

_____

_____

_____

2   This charity has a stock figure of £120,000 in the balance sheet. What is the quick ratio or acid test?

_____

_____

_____

3   Write down the ratio used to find the profit margin. It is expressed as a percentage (%).

_____

_____

_____

4   Which financial statement do you use to find the figures for the profit margin?

_____

5   What should you do to check if the profit margin is acceptable or a problem?

_____

_____

6   Write down the ratio you would use to find the return on capital employed from company accounts.

Return on capital employed = ————————— × 100

7 How do you work out 'capital employed'?

_____

_____

8 Why is the cash flow forecast a useful aid when measuring business performance?

_____

_____

_____

9 Why is it important to understand the business of the organization when measuring its performance?

_____

_____

_____

Answers to these questions can be found on page 96.

3 Summary

■ Financial indicators can be used to measure the business performance of an organization.

■ The indicators are usually expressed as ratios or percentages, and provide a guide to performance, particularly if we compare this year with previous years.

■ The indicators need to be compared to other companies in the same business or against an 'industry standard' in order to get a true picture of a particular business performance.

■ A cash flow forecast will provide helpful additional information about the solvency of an organization because it shows the **expected** performance, which can be compared with what is actually happening.

Session E
Sources of finance

1 Introduction

You've decided that a holiday would do you good. Corfu looks ideal but you've only saved £400 of the £900 cost. What can you do? You might ask the bank for an overdraft if you think you can repay it quickly, or perhaps a personal loan if it's going to take a year or more to pay back.

Organizations have similar problems. Any activity, and particularly any major investment, needs financing. If you work in a large organization your work area probably has a budget for expenditure each year. Perhaps additional money can be asked for in the case of major changes. But where does that money for the budget come from? And does it matter if the need is for the short term, say to cover an increase in credit allowed to continue, or the medium or long term?

In this session we'll look at the various ways in which finance can be obtained, and over what periods of time.

2 Funds available

Identifying sources of funds is the art of the possible. An organization's planning has to take into account how much finance is available and when. Public organizations particularly have money allocated annually; once the budget is spent, no more is available. This often leads to expenditure on projects early in the financial year and cut-backs at the end.

Some organizations have one budget for day-to-day expenditure such as wages and materials. This is a revenue budget. They have a capital budget for longer-term projects.

3 Short-term finance

In the holiday example in the introduction to this session we looked at savings and an overdraft. These are two common sources of short-term finance for organizations as well, although we call 'savings' retained profits. Organizations can also take advantage of trade credit, much as you or I might use the credit period allowed on a credit card to 'fund' our expenditure temporarily.

3.1 Retained profits

We saw earlier that retained profits (or accumulated surpluses in non-profit organizations) are built up through operations and are put into keeping organizations going on a day-to-day basis and in helping them grow. For instance, a manufacturing company may use £200,000 of materials in 2003 and use the profits generated from the sale of the goods manufactured from those materials to buy £250,000 of materials in 2004.

Retained profits are the major source of finance for businesses. One reason for this is that organizations do not have to pay interest or dividends to use retained profits. But, like money you put into a building society to earn interest, if you use it to buy something, you lose interest. Organizations ought to use money in the most effective way, so if they could earn more money investing in a bank deposit or building society account than in a new project, they should not use funds on that project.

Activity 38

5 mins

Organizations often use some money to pay day-to-day expenses such as wages while allowing customers one month's credit. Is this a good use of their money? Why?

_____

_____

I hope you will agree that providing credit is a good use of money because it generates more sales and profits above the cost of providing credit. So financing credit to customers is sensible using cheap retained profits, but would an overdraft be as effective?

3.2 Bank overdraft

Interest usually needs to be paid at high rates on an overdraft, so organizations would not wish to keep an overdraft at a high level for too long. However, overdrafts are useful for fluctuating, short-term needs.

Activity 39

5 mins

Pat runs a small chain of food shops and is charged VAT on some of the purchases that she makes for the shops. As she doesn't charge VAT to her customers she finds that she regularly reclaims the VAT that she paid on her purchases from the Customs and Excise Department (C & E). While she is waiting for payment from C & E at the end of each three month period, she often finds that she goes overdrawn at the bank. This overdraft is repaid in full when C & E pay.

Is this a good use of a bank overdraft? Explain your answer.

_____

_____

This is an ideal use of an overdraft because it is quickly repaid by the organization, so it does not have to pay much interest and the overdraft is used for a purpose that pays it back directly.

3.3 Trade credit

Stocks of material and utility bills are regularly financed by trade credit. Your organization is the customer of its various suppliers and they provide you with credit for the same reasons that you allow your customers credit.

Trade credit generally does not cost anything in the way of interest.

4 Medium-term and long-term finance

Organizations often need finance for a longer period than a few months (i.e. the short-term). Money may be needed now to be used up over, say, two years (the medium-term), or over several years (the long-term).

4.1 Retained profits

It should not be a surprise to you to meet retained profits again. You will have short-term, medium-term and long-term saving yourself. You might save up from your earnings for the deposit on a house, for a cruise to celebrate a big anniversary, or for retirement. Many organizations take a similar approach, by noting retained profit.

Activity 40

List **two** long-term projects that have been paid for by your organization through retained profits (or surpluses).

_____

_____

You may find it difficult to separate how much is provided from retained profits and how much from other sources in a pool of money for investment. Nevertheless you should have found that retained profits form a major part of the overall investment.

Another important source of finance is borrowing.

4.2 Loans

Sometimes money is not available from retained profits. There may be limited funds in the organization or the money may be tied up already. If this is the situation, and the organization has a promising new project, it may wish to borrow money.

Activity 41

3 mins

Linespar Ltd borrowed £20,000 from the bank for two years at an interest rate linked to market rates but currently quoted at 6 per cent. This is to finance a new project with a return estimated at 12 per cent (before interest on the loan).

Suggest **two** problems which might occur over the two years that could make the new project less attractive.

_____

_____

The return is purely an estimate. If the new project is not as successful as expected, the return may be less than projected. The company is looking for a net 6 per cent return, being the return on the new project less the interest charge, so it has little room for manoeuvre before it starts to make a loss.

In addition, the interest rate on the loan is linked to market rates and any changes in these could increase or decrease the profit from the new project.

All activities have some risk attached, but potential problems should be identified and allowed for. The new project described above is likely to be more viable if financed through retained profits.

Is funding through share capital different?

4.3 Share capital

> By purchasing shares, shareholders buy a financial interest in the organization. In return for their investment they may have voting rights and will expect part of the profits – dividends – in proportion to their shareholding.

Companies can raise capital through different kinds of share capital. Shareholders expect some income from their investment by way of dividends so, again, the expected return is important for any activity to be financed by shares.

Shares, or equity, finance is usually kept for very long-term investments because it is far more difficult to repay them than to pay back loans. In addition, public companies particularly are concerned to maintain investor confidence and maintain a good share price. They must make the best use of the finance.

Activity 42   5 mins

What would be the consequence for a company which financed a four-year project by shares, after which time the investment had been paid back two-fold?

_____

_____

_____

I hope you will agree that the company would have surplus money. Unless it could find another profitable source of investment for the cash it would only be able to invest it in banks, building societies, government and company investments. Usually this would provide a lower return than projects in the course of trade and might not pay the dividends that investors expected.

4.4 Grants

Many non-profit organizations, like charities and some others in the public sector, are financed by grants. These are funds which need not be paid back, generally providing certain conditions are fulfilled. However, to get the grants, organizations need to apply and convince the grant provider that the money is to be used appropriately. For instance, a branch of Age Concern might receive a grant of 50 per cent of the cost of a day centre if:

■ the local branch raised the other 50 per cent itself;
■ the project would meet the needs of, say, 25 people a day;
■ the day-to-day running of the project would be self-financing;
■ certain management and operational criteria are met.

Activity 43 · 5 mins

Suppose your organization agreed to provide a grant for a social club and provide grounds for sports. Suggest two ways in which the day-to-day running of the club could be self-financing.

_____

_____

Profits from the sale of food and drink are a common source of finance for social clubs. You might also have suggested membership fees, subscriptions, profits from dinner dances and other functions.

5 Flexible financing

Your organization may be short of funds but may need, say, a couple of additional vans to enable service staff to travel to customers and generate income from essential maintenance work.

The bank may not wish to lend any more to the organization and such investments are not appropriate for share issues and grants. Leasing and hire purchase offer the answer. The vans can be paid for at the same time as they are being used to earn money. After a period of time the organization may or may not own the vans but it will certainly have use of them.

Self-assessment 5

15 mins

1 a Name two types of short-term finance.

b Name two types of long-term finance.

2 Briefly explain why the interest rate charged on borrowing is important when deciding whether to finance a new project in this way.

3 Briefly explain when leasing may be a useful source of finance.

4 What makes retained profits a popular source of finance?

5 Homes for the Homeless is a charity which buys old houses, renovates them and provides them at a low rent for homeless families. Suggest how the charity would finance its work.

Answers to these questions can be found on pages 96–7.

6 Summary

- Organizations require finance even if it is repaid quickly. Some may require short-term finance and some finance for the medium or longer term.

- Short-term finance is used to meet day-to-day needs and can be supplied from retained profits, bank overdrafts and trade credit.

- Medium-term and long-term finance is provided from retained profits, share capital, loans and, generally in non-profit organizations, grants.

- If funds are not easily available, hire purchase or leases can be used if equipment and machinery can pay for regular payments from its operation.

- The cost of finance is important. The greater the cost of the finance, the greater the return needed from activities to meet the financing cost. Retained profits are generated from operations and are cheap. Ideally, organizations would wish to earn more from the use of retained profits than would be gained from putting the money into a bank deposit or building society account.

Performance checks

1 Quick quiz

Write down your answers in the space below to the following questions on *Understanding Finance*.

Question 1   Name the four ways in which money is said to be used.

_____

_____

_____

_____

Question 2   What are the three reasons why a business keeps accounting records and which are reflected in a balance sheet?

_____

_____

_____

Question 3   Name a financial statement which helps an organization plan for the future.

_____

_____

Question 4   Explain how profit is calculated.

_____

_____

Question 5   How is capital used in a business?

_____

_____

Question 6   Give the name for items purchased and kept in an organization for a long period. They are not intended for resale.

_____

Question 7   Explain what is meant by the term debtors.

_____

_____

_____

Question 8   Define working capital.

_____

Question 9   How can an organization anticipate when it will need to borrow money?

_____

_____

Question 10   Explain what is meant by depreciation.

_____

_____

_____

Question 11   What is the profit and loss account of a charity normaly called?

_____

_____

Question 12   Define capital employed.

_____

_____

Question 13   Write down the acid test calculation.

_____

_____

_____

Question 14   What is measured by the profit margin?

_____

_____

Question 15   What is meant by ROCE?

_____

_____

Question 16   State a source of both short-term and long-term funds.

_____

_____

Answers to these questions can be found on page 98.

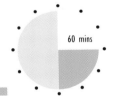

60 mins

2 Workbook assessment

Read through the following case incidents and then deal with the questions that follow, writing your answers on a separate sheet of paper.

Aeromotors Limited has been trading for a year and so it is time to draw up a profit and loss account and a balance sheet. (All amounts are in £'000.)

Sales for the year were £4,470. Stock at the beginning of the year was £130 and at the end of the year was valued at £500. Stock purchases during the year came to £3,000. Other expenses appearing in the profit and loss account were £1,000. Depreciation for the year was calculated at £240. The tax owed to the government is £200. The company owns a small area of freehold land valued at £1,100.

The equipment (cost less depreciation) is £200. Creditors total £600, and the bank balance is £30. Cash in the till is £20. There are debtors at £450. The car wash is owned by the company and its depreciated value is £600. The retained profit is £400. The company has not declared a dividend.

Use the financial information to produce the profit and loss account and the balance sheet, year ending 31 December.

When you have drawn up the financial statements, answer the questions about the analysis of performance.

You will need to separate out the items into those which appear in a profit and loss account and those which are found in a balance sheet.

Remember that the retained profit of £400 is transferred to the balance sheet from the profit and loss statement, so I suggest you produce the profit and loss account first and then the balance sheet.

Now answer the following questions.

1   What is the working capital in Aeromotors Limited?

2   What is the quick ratio or acid test based on this year's performance?

3   Why is the ratio important?

4   What is the capital employed in Aeromotors? (The capital employed is made up of fixed assets plus current assets less current liabilities.)

5   What is the return on the capital employed?

3 Work-based assignment

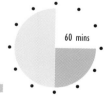

60 mins

Portfolio of evidence

S/NVQs B1.1, B1.2, D1.1, D1.2

The time guide for this assignment gives you an approximate idea of how long it is likely to take you to write up your findings. The result of your efforts should be presented on separate sheets of paper.

You will need to spend some additional time gathering information, talking to colleagues and thinking about the assignment. And, as you research and report, you should aim to develop your personal competency too. Remember that other people will be busy and that you may meet opposition against any ideas for change you may express. Be prepared for this so you are able to cope with such difficulties.

It is important that you establish a good working relationship with the people in accounts and finance who will, then, be more inclined to share information with you and help you interpret it. Perhaps you can help them in understanding your work area better too.

This assignment is in two parts.

I Speak to your manager or finance director, or your colleagues in the accounts office, and find out how the organization manages its cash flow. Explain your reasons for needing this information and that you will report back your findings.

If this is not possible, select some area of the work you are engaged in and see if you can identify roughly the cash flows that are involved, say for paying employees and their expenses, paying for raw materials and overheads, and paying occasionally for new fixed assets. In association with your manager or trainer, identify the periods of credit that your sector takes from suppliers and gives to customers. Then identify a sensible opening balance of cash. Again promise to report back to your manager or trainer.

a Draw up a cash flow forecast for the next three months, showing the cash received, the cash paid and the balance brought forward and carried forward each month. From your communications with others and your experience of the organization itself, do you think that cash flow is being effectively forecast and managed?

b Do operations generate cash? If day-to-day operations do not result in regular excesses of cash receipts over cash payments, how is this identified and managed? Is this the best way of identifying shortfalls, or can you suggest a better method? Alternatively, if the operations are cash generative and there is a regular or persistent excess of cash, how is this identified and managed? Is this the best way of identifying excesses, or can you suggest a better method?

c How are shortfalls of cash from operations funded? Is this the best way or can you suggest alternatives that would be more appropriate? Alternatively, how are excesses of cash used? Is this the best way or could you suggest alternatives that are more appropriate?

d From your experience of your organization's operations, do you consider that the organization forecasts its cash position effectively? What are the reasons for your conclusions?

e Write up a report, with a copy for the manager or trainer who helped you with the initial information. Explain your investigation and make any recommendations for change, with reasons, you consider would improve the performance and efficiency of your organization. Ensure that any recommendations you make pay regard to the sensitivity of those who have drawn up existing policies.

2 Try to obtain copies of your organization's year-end accounts, preferably for the current year and the previous two or three years.

Examine the profit and loss account and the balance sheet and read any accompanying notes.

a What was the retained profit? What was the increase or decrease in profit over the previous years, year on year?

b Use the knowledge you have gained to work out the current ratio and the profit margin ratio for your organization.

Talk over what you are doing with your manager and the accounts department. They will be interested in your work and may be able to help you if you have any difficulty with the way the annual accounts have been presented.

Discuss with them the financial situation of the business and try to find out why, for example:

- the profit margin ratio is at its present level;
- the organization retains profits and how these have been used over the last couple of years; ask about plans for the future;
- the current ratio is at its present level. Does it fluctuate over the year and why?

Talk over any ways you can think of that you and your work team may be able to improve the way in which your organization works.

Write up your findings and draw up an action plan for you and your work team. Discuss this with your manager.

If you are compiling an S/NVQ portfolio you may be able to use the output from this assignment as acceptable evidence. You should be able to refer to your search for information and the way you have used this information to help you form judgements and make decisions on the basis of collected facts.

Reflect and review

1 Reflect and review

Now that you'll have completed your work on *Understanding Finance*, let us review the workbook objectives.

You should be better able to:

■ understand how important it is for any organization to have sufficient cash.

Accountants seem to talk of everything as if it were money. You can see the good reasons for putting a money value on all things and activities in your place of work and generate financial information. By means of a circulating diagram called the business model, you have followed the use of cash in a business and seen where it goes and on what.

■ Remember that money is used to buy the assets of a business and to meet its liabilities. As a first line manager, you may be involved in bringing the fixed assets into operation and in using working capital. Are all these used in the most efficient way? Can you think of improvements you can suggest to your manager? Make notes of any matters that come to mind below.

_____

_____

_____

_____

_____

The second workbook objective was to:

- appreciate why it is vital for an organization to control its finances by forecasting and monitoring cash flow.

First of all we looked at the various source documents that are used in accounting records, from which accounts are in turn produced.

You may or may not have access to invoices, credit notes and receipts in your day to day work, but hopefully as a first line manager you can encourage your work team to be careful in preserving and passing on whatever source documentation does come your way.

We looked at the principles of forecasting cash flow and its control, and learned how important this is to the survival of an organization by completing a cash flow forecast.

You may or may not be involved in preparing or monitoring cash flow. Perhaps you can ensure that cash is not wasted by making sure that your work team minimizes waste.

The third workbook objective was to:

- identify appropriate providers of finance in given situations.

We have seen that the prime source of funds over whatever term is retained profits. These can be used to fund a short-term excess of expenditure over income due to, say, an extension of credit period for customers, but it can equally well be used to fund a long-term project which will generate profits well into the future. Other sources of short-term funds are overdrafts and extended trade credit. Sources of medium-term and long-term finance include loans, share capital and grants. Finally, flexible sources of finance such as leasing can be used in the medium and long term.

Try to find out how your organization funds short-term shortfalls in finance, and how new long-term projects are funded. What sort of return is made on all the funds used? Does this return vary depending on the type of finance? For instance, shareholders are often willing to take reduced dividends in return for retained profits being used to increase the value of the shares themselves over the medium and long term. Do you think the organization could make better use of the sources of funds that are available to it?

The fourth workbook objective was to:

- make sense of key financial information in profit and loss accounts and balance sheets.

Next we worked through the main aspects of drawing up profit and loss accounts (or income and expenditure accounts) and balance sheets. In this way we have extended the language of accountancy used in 'the business model' and you have worked with accountancy procedures. This should give you a better appreciation of the concerns of management in meeting the needs of investors and lenders.

- Perhaps management decisions which you had difficulties in understanding in the past now seem clearer. Think of a major change in your workplace which has been made recently. In general terms, how would you expect this to affect the profit and loss account (or income and expenditure account) and balance sheet of your organization?

_____

_____

_____

The final workbook objective was to:

- measure how well an organization is performing financially.

We have introduced financial analysis and you have learned to use some common tests of financial performance. Again you will see that the views of outsiders and management are influenced by the performance of the organization as shown by this information. Decisions are made with such points in mind.

- Take a look at the accounts of your business for the last couple of years and calculate the working capital and acid test ratios. What do these tell you about the trend between the two balance sheet dates? Make a note of any changes in policy which are likely to have led to the trend. If the position has been constant, is the level appropriate to the type of organization?

_____

_____

_____

_____

_____

2 Action plan

Use the plan on page 91 to develop further for yourself a course of action that is relevant to your task of understanding more about finance and the financial environment.

First, describe the outcome you would like to achieve as a result of the plan, and its expected benefits. Some possible outcomes you could identify are career advancement or improved efficiency of your work team. For example, you might like to suggest ways in which stock levels could be reduced, minimizing the costs of storage and possibilities of obsolescence. This would reduce both costs and help the organization run with less working capital. You would need to ensure that sufficient stock, of the correct types, is maintained to meet orders, so careful planning and liaison with your line manager would be important.

Alternatively, you may be thinking that you would like your own position to be reviewed. Perhaps if you had greater responsibility for the funds in your area of work or were involved more in consultations you feel you could be more effective. If so, how will you go about deciding what ought to be done and how will you persuade others of your ideas?

Make a note in the first column of the issues or problems, related to the outcome, which you think could arise. Then decide what you intend to do about each of them and make a note of your intended actions in Column 2. Try to anticipate questions which will be asked and have answers for them.

The resources you might need to implement any changes might include time, materials, information or money. You will need to estimate how much of each you will need and you may have to negotiate for some of them. In practical terms, the less you ask for, the more easily it is likely to be obtained, but there is little point in under-estimating your needs. This would not reflect well on the case you are making. Be realistic. Write down your resources in Column 3.

Your target completion dates should be entered in Column 4. After you have implemented your plan, write down the actual outcome.

Desired outcomes

1 Issues	2 Action	3 Resources	4 Target completion

Actual outcomes

3 Extensions

Extension 1

Book   *Sage Instant Accounting 2000*
Author   David Weale
Edition   1999 – supplied with disk
Publisher Babani Books

Book   *Simple and Practical Costing, Pricing and Credit Control*
Authors Keith Kirkland and Stuart Howard
Edition   1998
Publisher Kogan Page

Extension 2

Book   *The Business Plan Workbook*
Authors Colin Barrow, Paul Barrow and Robert Brown
Edition   4th Edition, 2001
Publisher Kogan Page (in association with *The Sunday Times*)

Extension 3

Book   *Business Accounting*
Authors Alan Sangster and Frank Wood
Edition   2002
Publisher Pearson Education

These extensions can be taken up via your ILM Centre. They will either have them or will arrange that you have access to them. However, it may be more convenient to check out the materials with your personnel or training people at work – they may well give you access. There are other good reasons for approaching your own people; for example, they will become aware of your interest and you can involve them in your development.

4 Answers to self-assessment questions

Self-assessment 1
on pages 16–17

1   In simple terms, companies keep accounting records to show what they own, owe and are owed. So suitable words would be:

    a   OWES to other people;
    b   OWED by other people;
    c   OWNS.

On the basis of these accounting records, the company can adjust what it is doing, so that it continues to make a profit and can plan what the business should do next. So the final responses should be along the lines of:

    d   PAID OUT to other people;
    e   PLAN for the future.

2   The following match and show money being used as:

    a   a medium of exchange, when (i) buying a bus ticket;
    b   a store of wealth, when (iii) contributing to a pension plan;
    c   a means of deferred payment, when (iv) buying a coat using a credit card;
    d   a measure of value, when having (ii) an antique clock valued at £750.

3   a   The surplus or profit of an organization is calculated by using the formula:

        Profit = Total income – Total expenditure

    b   Your two reasons why a business needs to make a profit could be selected from:

        ■ to survive;
        ■ to grow;
        ■ to reward investors and owners;
        ■ to replace machinery, equipment and so on.

4   a   Information on transactions in source documents is recorded in accounting records. These are then summarized in accounts, which allow the enterprise to see whether it is making a profit or surplus, and achieving its plans.

    b   1 Goods (net) total, VAT, invoice (gross) total, date/tax point.
        2 The same.
        3 The amount of the cheque.

Reflect and review

Self-assessment 2 on page 33

1   The items are matched as follows:

   a Owner's capital   (ii)   Capital provided by the business owner.
   b Fixed assets   (i)   Assets used within the business, and not intended for resale.
   c Working capital   (v)   Current assets less current liabilities.
   d Labour   (vi)   The cost to the business of its employees.
   e Overheads   (vii)   The incidental expenses incurred in running a business, including fuel and rent.
   f Debtors   (iv)   People who owe the business money.
   g Creditors   (iii)   People the business owes money to.

2   The most straightforward way to answer this question is to draw up a cash flow forecast.

	May £	June £
Opening capital	450	–
Receipts from sales	1,040	990
Receipts	1,490	990
Materials paid for	(500)	(560)
Overheads	(200)	(210)
Payments	(700)	(770)
Net cash	790	220
Balance B/F	Nil	790
Balance C/F	790	1,010

There is just enough money to buy the van for £1,000 but that would mean leaving the business very short of cash. Julia might be well advised to wait a little longer before making her purchase. Alternatively she could try to borrow money towards the cost of the delivery van which she could pay off over a longer period.

3   Offering customers a six month interest free credit period after previously allowing customers only one month credit means that the business will need to wait an extra five months for receipt for sales, and so will need to finance roughly five extra months' debtors. It is difficult to quantify this exactly, as some customers might not want to take up the offer and others might pay earlier than the six month period. In addition the business will be expecting the level of sales to increase so it will have to buy more stock to meet increased orders.

Together these factors will mean increased pressure on working capital with the figures for both stock and debtors increasing. Some of this may be offset by negotiating longer credit periods from suppliers, but the remaining squeeze on working capital will need to be financed. This may well mean negotiating an overdraft to tide the business over.

The benefits of making an offer like this are that the business is likely to generate more sales with existing and new customers which, providing all customers pay for what they order, means an increase in profits.

Self-assessment 3 on page 55–6

1   The profit and loss account should be as follows:

Lester Limited

Profit and loss account for the year ended 31 December

	£'000	£'000
Sales (352 + 400)		752
Cost of goods sold (20 + 520 − 70)		(470)
Gross profit		282
Overhead expenses		
Expenses	120	
Interest	12	
Depreciation	40	(172)
Profit before tax		110
Tax (110 × 20%)		(22)
Profit after tax		88
Dividend		(4)
Retained profit for the year		£84

---

2   a   Assets that are to be kept and used in the business are FIXED assets.

b   Assets that are expected to be turned into cash very soon are CURRENT assets.

Current assets are separated from fixed assets because a company needs to know how much cash it has, including items that it expects shortly to turn into cash.

So current assets are actual cash, plus goods for sale, money owed to the business, and so on, that will soon be turned into cash.

3 The items are described as follows:

    a Working capital is (ii) current assets less current liabilities.
    b Capital employed is (iv) long-term liabilities and owner's funds.
    c Depreciation is the (iii) amount written off the value of a fixed asset.
    d Balance sheet is a (i) statement in which assets equal liabilities.

Self-assessment 4 on page 67–8

1 $\dfrac{£240,000}{£400,000} = 0.6{:}1.$

2 $\dfrac{£240,000 - £120,000}{£400,000} = \dfrac{£120,000}{£400,000} = 0.3{:}1$

3 Profit margin $= \dfrac{\text{Profit before tax}}{\text{Sales revenue}} \times 100$

4 Profit and loss account.

5 Look back at the ratio for previous years, and compare the ratio with other companies. You may also be able to compare it against an 'industry standard'.

6 Return on capital employed $= \dfrac{\text{Profit before tax}}{\text{Capital employed}} \times 100$

7 Look at the balance sheet, work out the total assets and take away liabilities other than the owner's capital and reserves.

8 A cash flow forecast, where forecast figures are compared with actual figures, illustrates how successfully an organization is being run, particularly when meeting its debts.

9 Different types of business and organization typically have different ratios; it is meaningless to compare the performance of businesses in widely different industries.

Self-assessment 5 on page 78

1 a Types of short-term finance include bank overdraft, trade credit or retained profits.
    b Types of long-term finance include share capital, loans, grants or retained profits.

2 The interest rate charged on borrowing is important when deciding how to finance a new project because no project is worth undertaking if it costs more than its potential return. Also, the rate may not be fixed and may increase over the period of the project.

3 Leasing may be a useful source of finance when the machinery or equipment leased can be used to generate money to pay the finance charges when due.

4   Retained profits are a popular source of finance because no interest or dividends are payable on them. They are therefore a cheap source of finance.

5   Homes for the Homeless as a charity is likely to be eligible for grants to help them renovate the houses. As charities are non-profit organizations, they must rely on donations for their other finance needs. Some income will be provided by the low rents but this is unlikely to be enough to pay back the cost of property and renovation in a short period.

5 Answers to activities

**Activity 2
on pages 5–6**

Your completed accounts should look like this:

	What you are owed	What you owe
Monday	£ 60	£ 30
Tuesday	£ 60	£ 35
Wednesday	£ 60	£ 45
Thursday	£ 60	£ 40
Friday	£ 60	£ 10
Saturday	£ nil	£ 20
Sunday	£ nil	£ 10
Totals	£300	£190

Businesses tend to deal in larger sums but the principles are the same.

**Activity 23
on page 40**

You will probably have arrived at your figure for the cost of goods sold by adding £10,000 opening stock to £20,000 purchases, and taking away the closing stock of £5,000 to get £25,000.

Here is the profit and loss account of Straton Limited:

**Straton Limited
Profit and loss account for the year ended 31 March**

	£	£
Sales		60,000
Less cost of goods sold		(25,000)
Gross profit		35,000
Labour	15,000	
Overheads	10,000	(25,000)
Net profit		£10,000

6 Answers to the quick quiz

Answer 1   The four ways in which money is said to be used are: as a medium of exchange; as a store of wealth; as a means of deferred payment and as a measure of values.

Answer 2   The three reasons why a business keeps accounting records and which are reflected in a balance sheet are to know what it owes, to know what it is owed and to know what it owns.

Answer 3   Cash flow forecast. (Other forecasts can also be used.)

Answer 4   Profit = Total income less total expenditure.

Answer 5   Capital is used to purchase fixed assets and to provide working capital.

Answer 6   Fixed assets.

Answer 7   Debtors refer to the amounts outstanding from customers who are sold goods or services on credit, or to the customers themselves.

Answer 8   Working capital is current assets less current liabilities.

Answer 9   A cash flow forecast indicates when it is necessary to borrow money to meet liabilities.

Answer 10   Depreciation charges the cost of fixed assets to the profit and loss account over time.

Answer 11   An income and expenditure account.

Answer 12   Capital employed is total assets less liabilities **or** owner's capital plus retained profits.

Answer 13   Acid test $= \dfrac{\text{Current assets} - \text{Stock}}{\text{Current liabilities}}$

Answer 14   The profit margin measures the amount of net profit created from sales and is expressed as a percentage.

Answer 15   Return on capital employed.

Answer 16   Retained profits.

7 Certificate

Completion of this certificate by an authorized person shows that you have worked through all the parts of this workbook and satisfactorily completed the assessments. The certificate provides a record of what you have done that may be used for exemptions or as evidence of prior learning against other nationally certificated qualifications.

Pergamon Flexible Learning and ILM are always keen to refine and improve their products. One of the key sources of information to help this process are people who have just used the product. If you have any information or views, good or bad, please pass these on.

INSTITUTE OF LEADERSHIP & MANAGEMENT

SUPERSERIES

Understanding Finance

....

has satisfactorily completed this workbook

Name of signatory ....

Position ....

Signature ....

Date ....

Official stamp

Fourth Edition

INSTITUTE OF LEADERSHIP & MANAGEMENT
SUPERSERIES
FOURTH EDITION

To order – phone us direct for prices and availability details
(please quote ISBNs when ordering) on 01865 888190